Installing and Finishing
DRYWALL

DISCLAIMER

Those using this book must realize that the information presented was secured from a wide range of manufacturers, professional and trade associations, government agencies, and various architectural and engineering consultants and that in some cases generalized or generic examples are used. Every effort was made to provide accurate presentations. However, the author and the publisher assume no liability for the accuracy or applications shown. As the author and publisher have no control over how the reader chooses to utilize the information presented in this book and cannot determine the reader's level of proficiency or physical condition, they are not responsible for mishaps or other consequences that result from the reader's use of the information herein. It is essential that appropriate architectural and engineering staff be consulted and specific information about products be obtained directly from the manufacturer.

STERLING and the distinctive Sterling logo are registered trademarks of Sterling Publishing Co., Inc.

Library of Congress Cataloging-in-Publication Data

Spence, William Perkins, 1925-
  Installing and finishing drywall / William Spence.
    p. cm.
  Includes index.
  ISBN-13: 978-1-4027-4476-1
  ISBN-10: 1-4027-4476-5
  1. Drywall construction--Handbooks, manuals, etc. 2. Plastering--Handbooks, manuals, etc. I. Title.

TH8139.S65 2008
693'.6--dc22

                    2007030829

10 9 8 7 6 5 4 3 2 1

Published by Sterling Publishing Co., Inc.
387 Park Avenue South, New York, NY 10016
© 2008 by William Spence
Distributed in Canada by Sterling Publishing
c/o Canadian Manda Group, 165 Dufferin Street,
Toronto, Ontario, Canada M6K 3H6
Distributed in Canada by Sterling Publishing
Distributed in the United Kingdom by GMC Distribution Services
Castle Place, 166 High Street, Lewes, East Sussex, England BN7 1XU
Distributed in Australia by Capricorn Link (Australia) Pty. Ltd.
P.O. Box 704, Windsor, NSW 2756, Australia

Book design and layout: Cecile Kaufman

Printed in China

Sterling ISBN-13: 978-1-4027-4476-1
        ISBN-10: 1-4027-4476-5

For information about custom editions, special sales, premium and corporate purchases, please contact Sterling Special Sales Department at 800-805-5489 or specialsales@sterlingpublishing.com.

Installing and Finishing

DRYWALL

William P. Spence

STERLING

New York / London
www.sterlingpublishing.com

Contents

Part III
Finishing Drywall   85

Preface

DRYWALL INSTALLATION AND finishing is a task undertaken by many who enjoy doing some of the work on their home—be it a repair or a new addition. It is also a service provided by skilled craftsmen. It requires strength, ability to plan and execute the plan, ethical attitudes toward proper installation, and highly skilled finishing ability.

This book provides a look at the basic materials, installation techniques, and finishing procedures for drywall work. If these procedures and guidelines are carefully followed, a person can do a good job of installation and finishing. The craftsman will do the job much faster, but the homeowner, while slow, can handle smaller projects.

Part 1 of the book alerts you to the importance of building codes and then illustrates the installation tools in common use. It gives details about the most commonly used drywall panels and fasteners and concludes with a simple method for estimating the materials needed.

Part 2 gets into the actual installation techniques and methods, including some special wall and ceiling covering problems. It concludes by showing some of the types of trim and corner beads most frequently used, and explains how to install them.

Part 3 relates to finishing the walls and ceiling after the drywall has been installed. It alerts you to the common defects that require correction. The most frequently used finishing tools and materials are discussed, and the techniques for finishing joints, trim, and corner bead are covered in detail. Since textured ceilings are popular, an entire chapter is devoted to hand- and spray-texturing and other finishing techniques commonly used.

William Spence

Tools and Materials PART I

Building Codes and Inspections

BOTH RESIDENTIAL AND commercial construction must meet the requirements of local building codes. A building code is a published code, established by the local government, that sets forth regulations for building practices, materials, and installations in order to protect the health, welfare and safety of the public. The architect is responsible for recording construction details so that the building meets the code. This includes all factors related to the installation and finishing of drywall. As the drywall contractor, it is imperative that your work proceeds as set forth by the architect; if areas appear to not meet local codes, you should discuss this with the general contractor.

Building Codes

Most localities have adopted the International Residential Code for One- and Two-Family Dwellings (IRC) (**1–1**). It is a comprehensive, stand-alone residential code that establishes regulations for one- and two-family dwellings and townhouses. It is founded on broad-based principles that make possible the use of new materials and new building designs. The IRC is published by the International Code Council, 4051 West Flossmore Road, Country Club Hills, Illinois 60478. The development of this code has replaced the longstanding codes promulgated by BOCA (BOCA National Building Codes),

ICBO (Uniform Building Codes), and SBCCI (Standard Building Codes).

The detailed requirements for interior wall finish using gypsum wallboard are found in Chapter 7, *Wall Covering in the International Residential Code for One- and Two-Family Dwellings.* This specifies for various thicknesses of gypsum wallboard the maximum spacing of framing members, the maximum spacing of fasteners, and the sizes of nails and screws for wood framing.

The International Building Code (IBC) establishes minimum regulations for building systems using prescriptive

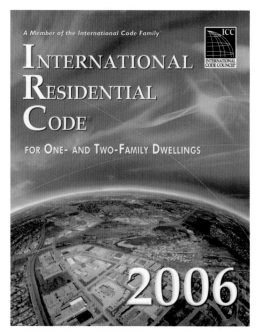

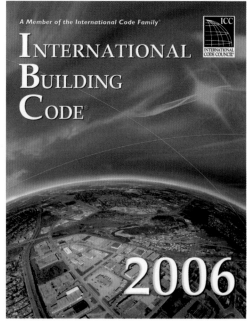

▲ **1–1.** *The International Residential Code for One- and Two-Family Dwellings* is a comprehensive code that establishes residential regulations for all parts of the United States. *(2006 International Residential Code for One- and Two-Family Dwellings, copyright 2006, Falls Church, Virginia: International Code Council. Reproduced with permission. All rights reserved. ww.iccsafe.org)*

▲ **1–2.** *The International Building Code* is a comprehensive code that establishes minimum regulations for building systems, using prescriptive and performance-related provisions. *(2006 International Building Code, Copyright 2006, Falls Church, Virginia: International Code Council. Reproduced with permission. All rights reserved. www.iccsafe.org)*

and performance-related provisions (**1–2**). It was founded on broad-based principles that make possible the use of new materials and new building designs. It provides a model code development process that offers an international forum of building professionals to discuss performance and prescriptive code requirements. It encourages international consistency in the application of provisions. Chapter 25, *Gypsum Board and Plaster,* details the recommendations for these materials.

The International Building Code continues to develop and maintain the model codes promulgated by BOCA National Codes, ICBO Uniform Building Codes and SBCCI Standard Codes. It is a copyrighted work of the International Code Council.

The American Society for Testing and Materials (ASTM) establishes standard specifications for many of the materials used in construction. These specifications are used in the United States and are referred to by a number such as ASTM C36, which is the standard for gypsum wallboard. In **Table 1–1** are examples of standards related to gypsum wallboard and accessories.

TABLE 1–1
Gypsum Board Materials & Accessories

Material	Standard*
Gypsum sheathing	ASTM C79
Gypsum wallboard	ASTM C36
Joint reinforcing tape for Gypsum	ASTM C474; C475
Nails for gypsum board	ASTM C514
Steel screws	ASTM C1002; C954
Water-resistant gypsum backing board	ASTM C630

* Standard developed by the American Society for Testing and Materials

Building Inspection

The local government will have a department responsible for inspecting buildings under construction. You should remember that the drywall covers up the electrical system, the plumbing system, and a lot of the mechanical system. Before you start to work, be certain the general contractor has had all of these systems inspected. You do not want to cover up anything until the inspections have been complete. One way to tell is to check the on-site building inspection sheet. It is posted on the site for all to see. The building inspectors sign it when an inspection, such as electrical, has been completed and the work is found to be according to code (1–3).

BUILDING INSPECTORS

Since your local building inspectors are more familiar with the codes than you probably are, a visit with them during an inspection or a call to them with questions will help you to learn a lot about how they read and interpret the code and what they expect when they come on the job. Most inspectors hope the job is finished correctly so they can approve it and move on to the next job. They get no pleasure out of having to reject a job and

make a return visit. They can also make suggestions about how to correct a defect or do the job better next time.

When checking the drywall, the inspector looks for things like the proper placement of the drywall panels, adequate nailing, and completed installation of the required fire-wall covering.

You should be aware that with the development of the International Codes there may be some changes in the local codes that can influence how you do a job.

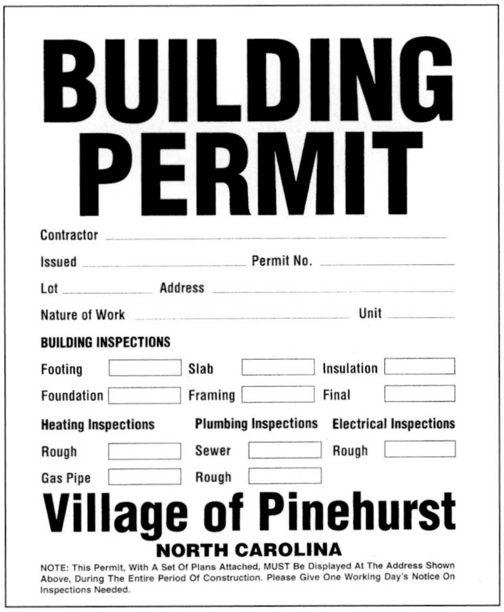

BUILDING PERMIT

Contractor _____

Issued _____ Permit No. _____

Lot _____ Address _____

Nature of Work _____ Unit _____

BUILDING INSPECTIONS

Footing [   ]   Slab [   ]   Insulation [   ]

Foundation [   ]   Framing [   ]   Final [   ]

Heating Inspections   **Plumbing Inspections**   **Electrical Inspections**

Rough [   ]   Sewer [   ]   Rough [   ]

Gas Pipe [   ]   Rough [   ]

Village of Pinehurst
NORTH CAROLINA

NOTE: This Permit, With A Set Of Plans Attached, MUST Be Displayed At The Address Shown Above, During The Entire Period Of Construction. Please Give One Working Day's Notice On Inspections Needed.

◄ **1–3.** This permit, issued by the local government, must be posted on the jobsite. *(Courtesy Village of Pinehurst, North Carolina)*

2

Installation Tools

TOOLS YOU WILL NEED *to hang gypsum board are few, but should be of the highest quality. Speed is important, and high-quality tools will yield a faster and better result. For installation you will need tools for measuring and layout, cutting, nailing, screwing, lifting, and hole cutting, as well as some type of bench or platform.*

Measuring and Layout Tools

You will use various measuring tools to mark the length and width of panels and layout angles.

TAPE MEASURE

A tape measure of good quality, usually 12 to 25 feet long, is required. Measuring tapes are used a great deal and are subject to hard wear and bending. Two types are available. One is a standard metal tape and the other is an electronic tape. The electronic tape has a digital readout which makes it a lot easier and faster to use (**2–1** and **2–2**).

◀ **2–1.** A 25-ft. steel tape is frequently used for measuring and cutting drywall. *(Courtesy L.S. Starrett Company)*

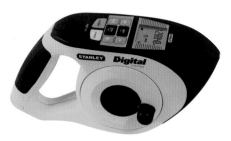
◀ **2–2.** This digital tape measures distances up to 1,500 feet and displays dimensions in feet, inches, meters, or centimeters. *(Courtesy Stanley Tools)*

▲ **2–3.** This drywall T-square has a 48-inch-long blade. It is used for measuring layout angles and as a guide for cutting panels.

T-SQUARE

The drywall T-square (2–3) is used to lay out cuts on the surface of the panel. These can be 90-degree cuts and angles. In addition it can be used as a guide for cutting the panel with a utility knife, as shown in 2–4. (See Chapter 5 for additional information.)

LEAD PENCIL

A soft lead pencil is best for marking on gypsum panels. It should be kept light. Never use ballpoint pens. If any of the line shows after taping, it will bleed through almost any type of paint put over it.

STUD FINDERS

It is often necessary to locate a stud or joist behind a drywall panel. A rather ineffective way is to tap on the panel until you get a solid sound and then drill a small-diameter test hole to see if you hit

a stud. This is time consuming and often several holes have to be drilled. The best technique is to use a stud finder. There are three types of stud finders generally available. These are magnetic, ultrasonic, and electronic stud finders.

The **magnetic stud finder** has a magnet that rotates on a pin. As it is moved across the wall and passes over a nail, the magnet swings toward the nail. The nail, if properly installed, should be in the center of the stud. The stud can then be located by moving vertically from this nail. Since studs are typically located 16 to 24 inches apart, measure over to locate the next one. Use the stud finder to verify the location. Remember that stud spacing will differ around doors, windows, corners, and other intersections. Of the three types, this type of stud finder is not the best choice.

The **ultrasonic stud finder** produces ultrasonic waves that sense the change in density of the wall behind it. As the stud finder crosses a stud, the density increases and allows accurate location of the sides of the stud or joist, giving the actual width.

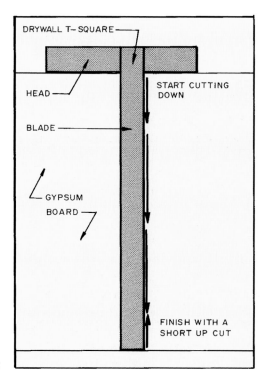

DRYWALL T–SQUARE

HEAD

BLADE

GYPSUM BOARD

START CUTTING DOWN

FINISH WITH A SHORT UP CUT

◀ **2–4.** How to direct the utility knife when cutting drywall panels.

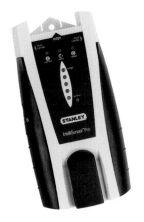

▲ **2–6.** A utility knife is an excellent tool to use for scoring drywall. *(Courtesy Stanley Tools)*

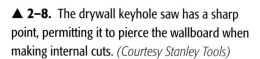

▲ **2–8.** The drywall keyhole saw has a sharp point, permitting it to pierce the wallboard when making internal cuts. *(Courtesy Stanley Tools)*

▲ **2–5.** This stud finder differentiates wood, metal, and live wire through drywall and many other wall materials. An LED display and an audio horn indicate the stud edge. *(Courtesy Stanley Tools)*

▲ **2–7.** The drywall saw is hardened and tempered for long wear. *(Courtesy Stanley Tools)*

The **electronic stud finder** is also more accurate than the magnetic finder (**2–5**). It may have a light or make a beep that is activated when it passes over metal such as a nail or steel stud or joist.

Cutting Tools

Cutting gypsum board is very hard on tools. They must be designed for this purpose. You will find that a saw designed to cut wood does not stay sharp very long on gypsum board. Following are the most frequently used tools.

UTILITY KNIFE

The utility knife is an inexpensive but sharp cutting tool. Most come with a supply of replaceable cutters in the handle, and additional cutters can be purchased at your hardware store. Do not use a dull blade. It can lead to a slip and a cut hand or leg (**2–6**).

SAWS

A drywall saw (**2–7**) is used to make straight cuts, and the drywall keyhole saw (**2–8**) can make curved cuts and various openings in a panel, as for an

electrical outlet box. The tip of the keyhole saw is very sharp and is used to penetrate the panel so a cut can be made. Place the tip against the panel and rotate it, cutting a hole through it. Then begin a sawing action to form the opening desired.

In addition to the two handsaws that are standard equipment when hanging drywall, it will be useful to have on hand an electric saber saw (**2–9**). This basic

▲ **2–9.** The electric saber saw rapidly cuts wallboard and is especially good for making internal cuts.

▲ **2–10.** The circle cutter has a hardened steel cutting blade and cuts through the face paper or mesh to score the gypsum core. *(Courtesy Kraft Tool Company)*

power handtool can become indispensable for making quick and accurate cuts in wallboard. The up-and-down blade action is especially good for making internal cuts, both straight and curved, that need to be precise.

CIRCLE CUTTER

A circle cutter is used to score through the paper and into the gypsum (**2–10**). The pivot is inserted into the panel at the center of the hole. The cutting wheel is moved out a distance equal to the radius of the circle, and then is rotated about the center as it is pressed into the panel. It should cut the paper and score the gypsum core. After removing the circle cutter, knock out the scored circle with a hammer. Use your utility knife to smooth out and clean up the hole on the rear of the panel.

RASPS

Various types of rasps are used to smooth the rough edges of a panel after it has been cut. The most effective is the perforated-blade type of surface-forming tool (**2–11**). These rasps are available in a range of sizes. The blade is removed and replaced when it becomes dull.

ROUTER

A drywall router—also referred to as the power hole saw—is used to cut openings in the panel. The center of the hole, such as for an electrical outlet box, is marked. The drill bit enters at this point and is moved until it hits the side of the box. It is then guided around the sides, cutting away the gypsum board as it moves (**2–12**). (Refer to Chapter 5 for additional information.)

STRIPPER

A gypsum board stripper is shown in **2–13**. It is used to cut long, narrow strips of gypsum board such as those often needed around door or window openings. When these are cut with a utility knife, they frequently will crack. The handle serves as a guide and runs along the edge of the panel. The cutter is set in the distance desired. The maximum width is 4½ inches.

Nailing and Screwdriving Tools

You have the choice of manual- or power-operated nailing and screwdriving tools. Power-operated tools drive nails and staples much faster than a hammer. Screws are always driven with some type of power screwdriving tool.

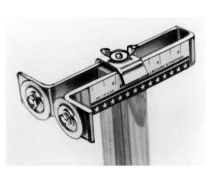

▲ **2–13.** The drywall stripper is used to cut long, narrow strips of wallboard. *(Courtesy Kraft Tool Company).*

▲ **2–11.** This is one type of a wide variety of rasps that can be used to smooth the edges of the wallboard. *(Courtesy Kraft Tool Company)*

▲ **2–12.** This electric hole saw uses a variety of spiral bits to penetrate the wall material and cut an opening in drywall, wood, composites, plastics, vinyl siding, and other such materials. *(Courtesy Bosch Power Tools and Accessories, Rotozip Tools).*

▲ **2–14.** Each of these drywall hammers has a serrated face that keeps it on the nail. They are available in several weights and handle lengths. *(Courtesy Kraft Tool Company)*

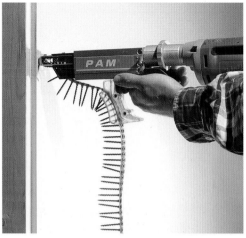

▲ **2–16.** This electric screwdriver is equipped with a strip-collated screw system that enables the gypsum board installer to quickly position and install the screw. It has a lock-in calibrated depth control. *(Courtesy PAM Fastening Technology, Inc.)*

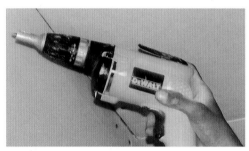

▲ **2–15.** Screws are driven with an electric screwdriver.

DRYWALL HAMMER

The drywall hammer is used to pry and jack the wallboards into the desired position. It has a notch which is used to pull nails (**2–14**), and its face is serrated with grooves at a 90-degree angle to help it from slipping off the head of the nail. Its face is also rounded to create a dimple depression in the drywall as the nail is set, and this depression is filled with joint compound to cover the nail head. The nail head has a dull rounded edge.

ELECTRIC SCREWDRIVER

An electric screwdriver (also called a *screwgun*) is used to drive drywall screws through the panel into wood and metal studs (**2–15**). It has a magnetic screw-

holding tip and an adjustable nosepiece. The nose-piece is used to adjust a clutch. The clutch controls the amount of torque available to drive the screw, and this is adjusted to release and stop the driving of the screw when it has reached the proper degree of tightness (the head of the screw should be just below the surface of the panel but should not tear the paper or crush the gypsum core).

An automatic screwdriving attachment is available that fits most electric screwdrivers (**2–16**). It has a series of 50 screws on a collated strip that automatically positions them in the chuck for rapid driving.

CLINCH-ON TOOL

Another device that is used in some areas is the clinch-on tool (**2–17**). It fits over the metal corner bead, is struck with a mallet, and forces metal teeth to crimp the edge of the metal bead into the drywall.

▲ **2–17.** The clinch-on tool is placed against the metal corner bead. The protruding face is struck with a mallet, forcing the prongs to pierce the bead and bend metal prongs into the drywall. *(Courtesy Kraft Tool Company)*

INSTALLATION TOOLS

▲ **2–18.** Power staplers are available that can drive a wide range of staple sizes and wire diameters. *(Courtesy Porter-Cable)*

STAPLERS

Various types of staplers are used to attach corner beads. They must be powerful enough to drive the staple through the gypsum panel and into the stud (**2–18**). They may be either manually activated or air-powered.

POWER NAILERS

Some types of air-powered nailers can be used to hang gypsum board. They are operated by pressing the tool firmly against the panel and squeezing the trigger. They will not work unless the tool is held firmly against the work. You have to adjust it until the nail is driven firmly in place, producing the required dimple in the surface of the panel.

Lifting Tools and Working Platforms

Much of the work involved in installing drywall panels will be above the floor. This requires the use of sturdy trestles, benches, and scaffolds. Be certain they are in good repair and properly assembled. They must stand squarely on the floor. All debris in the area must be removed. The working platforms should be kept clean of dropped compound, which means frequent cleaning. It is necessary to wear sturdy shoes with soles that will not slip. Since ceiling work requires you to use both hands over your head, a good solid footing is essential.

TRESTLES, BENCHES, AND SCAFFOLDS

Most ceilings in residential construction are 8 feet high. The installer and finisher can work on them from a trestle or drywall bench that is at least 2 feet high. The trestle in **2–19** allows the height of the plate to be adjusted. A certified plank is supplied with them so the load-carrying capacities are ensured. A metal framed drywall bench is shown in **2–20**. While the height is not adjustable, you are assured it will carry two installers safely.

In commercial buildings, it is often necessary to erect a full scaffolding. It is best to use a manufactured product

▼ **2–19.** These ladder-type trestles permit the height of the scaffold board to be adjusted as needed. *(Courtesy Wing Enterprises, Inc.)*

▲ **2–20.** This sturdy drywall bench will provide a reliable support, but the platform must be kept clean.

▲ **2–21.** This manufactured pipe scaffolding provides a wide-base, sturdy work platform. The wood planks used should be certified for use as scaffold planking.

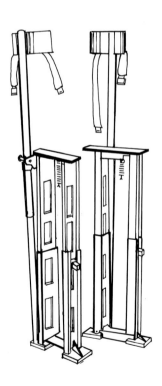

▲ **2–22.** Stilts can be used instead of scaffolding to reach the ceiling and upper walls. The applicator has the mobility to move about as required.

(2–21). They are structurally sound and easily erected, and they are made to meet the regulations established by the federal government under the Occupational Safety and Health Act (OSHA). OSHA has manuals detailing the requirements for scaffolding.

STILTS

Stilts are worn by the finish applicator; they give him full mobility and the height needed to reach normal ceilings. It takes some practice to get used to walking on them (2–22). They can be adjusted for different heights.

LIFTING TOOLS

The two commonly used devices to assist in lifting and placing panels are the drywall lifter and the panel lifter. The drywall lifter is placed under the edge of the gypsum panel as it leans against the wall and rests on the floor. The tail is pushed down, raising the panel an inch or so until it butts against the top wall panel already installed (2–23). Keep the lifter near the center of the panel so that both ends will rise evenly. The panel lifter will hold the entire gypsum panel, raise it up against the wall or ceiling, and then hold it there while it is being nailed (2–24).

Safety Guidelines

Installing and finishing drywall creates a number of situations where health hazards exist and personal safety equipment must be worn. The process creates dust and larger particles in the air, so safety glasses with side shields are required (2–25). When sanding or cutting drywall, a disposable dust mask or one with replaceable filters should be worn (2–26). Wear heavy leather work shoes that have non-slip soles, not canvas sneakers. Keep a pair of heavy leather work gloves handy (2–27) to use when installing scaffolding and moving

▲ **2–24.** Full panels can be lifted into place on the wall or ceiling with a panel lifter. *(Courtesy Panelift® Brand Drywall Lift, Courtesy Telpro Inc.)*

▲ **2–23.** A drywall lifter will lift and hold the bottom panel in place while you nail it. *(Courtesy Kraft Tool Company)*

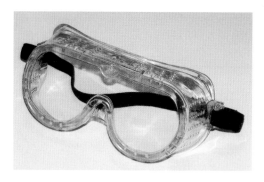

▲ 2–25. Safety glasses are an essential piece of personal protection equipment.

▲ 2–26. This type of dust mask is widely used. However, buy only those marked NIOSH-approved. Some appear to be similar but are not effective.

sheets of drywall. It is advisable to wear a hard hat and on many job sites they are required to meet government safety regulations. Lack of proper safety equipment can lead to a fine. The Occupational Safety and Health Administration (OSHA) Act provides minimum safety and health standards for working conditions. Construction occupations are one of the leading sources of injuries and deaths among industrial workers.

▲ 2–27. Wear heavy gloves when handling scaffolding and large quantities of drywall panels.

Drywall Panels and Fasteners

3

GYPSUM DRYWALL PANELS *have been in use for many years and are the standard interior wall and ceiling finish material. In addition, they have exterior applications, are a major fire-retardant material, and are used to control the flow of sound through walls, floors, and ceilings.*

Gypsum wallboard is installed dry, which is why it came to be called drywall. Drywall is easier to install and costs less than plaster walls, which require a base material plus several layers of wet plaster.

The panels are formed with a gypsum core between layers of a specially formulated paper. On the face is a strong smooth-surfaced paper that will be finished with paint, wallpaper, or some other material. The back has a strong natural-finish paper. The paper is folded around the long edges of the panel and the ends are square-cut and smooth, revealing the gypsum core.

The fire-resistant properties of gypsum wall board are due to the fact that gypsum will not burn and the water in it is released as steam, enabling it to remain intact until all the water has been removed. The panel then fails because the gypsum has been calcined (roasted).

The gypsum panel, while resisting fire, also reduces the passage of heat to the other side of the panel. This reduces the possibility that wood on the back side of the panel will ignite. Fire-resistant wall designs are available from various manufacturers. One- and two-hour fire ratings are common (3–1). A special drywall product, Type-X gypsum, is designed for areas where a high fire resistance is mandated by building codes.

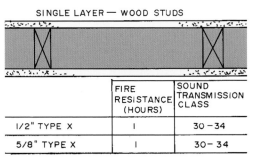

	FIRE RESISTANCE (HOURS)	SOUND TRANSMISSION CLASS
1/2" TYPE X	1	30 – 34
5/8" TYPE X	1	30 – 34

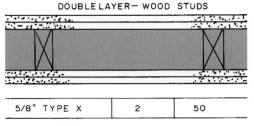

5/8" TYPE X	2	50

▲ **3–1.** Fire resistance ratings for several frequently used gypsum drywall installations.

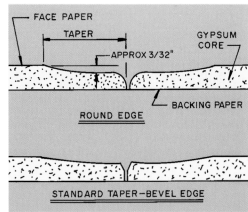

▲ **3–2.** Two of the types of tapered panel edges commonly available.

The gypsum core is composed of a mineral rock called gypsum. The basic mineral is calcium sulfate, chemically combined with water to become crystallized. The rock is mined, crushed, and ground to the fineness of flour. It is calcined (roasted) which drives off some of the chemically combined water as steam. The calcined gypsum is then mixed with water and sandwiched between two sheets of specially manufactured paper-forming the gypsum wallboard panel.

Gypsum drywall panels are sold two to a package. They are held together with a tape edge. This is stripped off, separating the two panels. These double panels are quite heavy. Two ½-inch panels will weigh 109 pounds and two ⅝-inch panels weigh 147 pounds.

Gypsum Wallboard

There are many types of gypsum wallboard available. Manufacturers have catalogs giving detailed technical information about the properties and uses of each. The following types are frequently used. Specific details will vary depending upon the company that manufactures the panels. General technical information is shown in **Table 3–1**.

REGULAR GYPSUM WALLBOARD

Regular gypsum wallboard is an economical product to use to finish interior walls and ceilings. The panels have a noncombustible core composed of gypsum and some additives, so it provides some fire protection. It also has sound deadening properties. Regular gypsum has a paper covering on the front, back, and the long edges, which may be tapered or have some other profile (**3–2**). The ends are cut square and the gypsum is visible. It is installed on wood and metal framing members, and the joints are finished with special tape and finishing compounds.

Following are typical uses for regular gypsum wallboard: ¼- to ⅜-inch-thick is generally used for remodeling jobs, two-layer installations, and curved walls and ceilings; and ½- to ⅝-inch is generally used on all interior walls and ceilings.

TABLE 3–1
Data for Various Types of Gypsum Wallboard

Type	Thickness (inches)	Width (feet)	Length (feet)
Regular	¼, ½, ⅜, ⅝	4	6–16
Type X (fire-resistant)	½, ⅝	4	6–16
Moisture-resistant	½ reg., ⅝ type X	4	6–16
Flexible	¼	4	8 & 10
High-strength ceiling	½	4	6–16
Pre-decorated	½	4	8, 9 & 10
Sound deadening	¼	4	8
Sheathing	½, ⅝	4	8, 9 & 10
Soffit	½, ⅝	4	8–12
Paperless	½, ⅝	4	8

FIRE-RESISTANT GYPSUM WALLBOARD

Fire-resistant gypsum wallboard is identified as a Type-X panel. The gypsum core and paper covering the front, back, and edges are treated with additives that increase the resistance to fire. They are used to meet the fire code requirements for fire-resistant construction and prevent rapid transfer of heat to the structural members. The core contains considerable moisture that evaporates when the panel is subjected to heat. This retards the passage of heat until the moisture is gone. The core contains noncombustible fibers that help it continue resisting penetration by fire even after the moisture is gone. Multiple layers can be installed to increase the amount of time it will retard the passage of fire. Typical applications include walls between a garage and the house or a common wall between apartments.

MOISTURE-RESISTANT GYPSUM WALLBOARD

Moisture-resistant gypsum wallboard has a specially formulated gypsum core, and is designed to serve as the base for the installation of ceramic tile and other nonabsorbent wall finish materials. The core and facing materials are treated to withstand the effects of moisture and humidity. One type has a moisture-resistant core covered with a treated, water-resistant paper on both sides. The face paper is green, which helps identify this as a moisture-resistant panel (3–3). The water-resistant tile adhesive is applied over the wall covering, the nail heads, and joints between the panels. The wall area that won't be tiled is taped and finished using normal drywall tapes and compounds.

WATER-RESISTANT GYPSUM WALLBOARD

Another product is water-resistant gypsum tile-backer panel. It has a treated, water-resistant core with glass mats on the front and back and a gray heat-cured acrylic coating on the face side to which the tile is bonded. The joints are covered with the manufacturer-recommended, self-adhesive glass-fiber mesh tape.

▲ **3–3.** This bathtub area has been fiber-covered with moisture-resistant gypsum wallboard. It has a moisture-resistant core covered with treated, water-resistant paper on both sides. It is often referred to as green board.

CEILING WALLBOARD

A high-strength ½- and ⅝-inch-thick gypsum panel is available for use on ceilings. It has a special treated core that helps the panel resist sagging over time.

FLEXIBLE GYPSUM DRYWALL

Flexible gypsum wallboard is designed for finishing curved surfaces such as archways, curved walls and ceilings, and curved stairways. It will bend to both concave and convex surfaces. It is typically ¼ inch thick and is usually applied in double layers. It has a fire-resistant core encased in heavy natural finish paper on the face side and a strong liner paper on the back. It is best installed with the long edge perpendicular to the wall studs.

VINYL-SURFACED GYPSUM WALLBOARD

Vinyl surfaced gypsum wallboard is a pre-finished product offering a variety of colors and patterns. This eliminates the need for additional finishing steps or painting after it has been installed. It is very abrasion resistant and common dirt and marks can be removed by wiping with a moist cloth or sponge and mild soap. Stubborn stains can be removed by rubbing the surface with a bristle brush and a solvent such as mineral spirits or denatured alcohol.

HIGH-IMPACT GYPSUM WALLBOARD

High-impact gypsum wallboard is designed for use where the wall is likely to be subject to occasional impact or penetration. It has a fire-resistant, Type-X gypsum core enclosed in heavy paper and a polycarbonate film on the back side.

FOIL-BACKED GYPSUM WALLBOARD

This type of product consists of a fire-resistant gypsum core encased in heavy, natural-finish paper on the face side and a strong liner paper on the backside to which aluminum foil is laminated. It is used on exterior walls and ceilings. The aluminum foil serves as a vapor barrier to help keep the interior moisture inside the building at a suitable level.

PAPERLESS GYPSUM WALLBOARD

This type of panel is made with glass mats bonded to the gypsum core, replacing the traditional paper facing. They are used on interior walls where there is the possibility that moisture or humidity in the room could cause mold to form such as the walls in a bathroom. Should they get accidentally wet, they will not be damaged as would regular gypsum wallboard. The joints are covered with fiberglass joint tape and finished with setting-type joint compound. They can then be finished in the same way as regular gypsum wallboard.

GYPSUM SHEATHING

Gypsum sheathing is a water-resistant panel used on the exterior of walls as an underlayment for exterior siding such as wood, vinyl, and brick. It is attached directly to the studs. One type has a wax-treated water-resistant core that is covered with a water-repellent paper on both sides and on the long edges. It is available with a Type-X fire-resistant core. It is also used as sheathing on steel-framed commercial buildings. Many codes do not require it to be covered with a layer of building felt.

Another type of gypsum sheathing has a moisture-resistant, fire-resistant, gypsum core that resists the growth of mold. It has glass mats on both sides that resist moisture and mold. It has shear values similar to those of wood fiberboard when installed as directed by the manufacturer.

GYPSUM SOFFITS

Gypsum soffit board is a moisture-resistant fire-resistant panel used on residential and commercial soffits. It is covered on both sides with a water-repellent paper. The core has additives to increase the sag resistance of the panel. It is installed over wood and metal framing. Manufacturer-supplied tapes and compounds are used on the joints between panels. The exposed surface should be painted with two coats of an alkyd-base exterior paint.

CEMENT BOARD

Cement board is not a gypsum product, but is widely used to cover walls in areas, such as showers, where the wall is directly exposed to water. The panels are covered with ceramic tile. The panels have a cement core covered with a fiber-glass mesh (3–4). One side is smooth, and the other rough. The rough side is exposed, and the ceramic tile is bonded to it with thin-set mortar. If an adhesive is to be the bonding agent, the smooth side is the exposed face. Sizes are shown in **Table 3–2**. Cement board is secured to wood studs with manufacturer-supplied, galvanized, 1¼-inch wood screws or 1½-inch galvanized roofing nails spaced 8 inches O.C. Fasten cement board to steel framing with 1¼-inch manufacturer-supplied, galvanized steel screws spaced 6 inches O.C.

▲ **3–4.** Cement board has a cement core covered with fiberglass mesh. It serves as a water-resistant base upon which ceramic tiles can be installed.

Drywall Nails

The two basic types of nails used to secure drywall to wood studs are annular ring nails and cement-coated nails. Annular ring nails hold the best and reduce the tendency for nails to pop out through the finished wall. Nails may have flat or concave heads that are thin at their outer rim. Specially colored nails are used to secure predecorated panels. They have a very small head, and are supplied by the drywall manufacturer (3–5).

You should be certain to use nails of the proper length. Annular ring nails must penetrate the stud at least ⅞ inch and cooler nails 1⅛ inches. Type X gypsum panels require longer nail

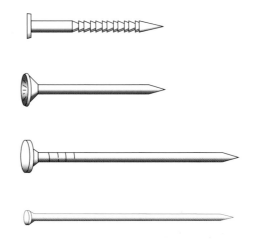

▲ **3–5.** Nails commonly used to secure gypsum panels to wood framing.

TABLE 3–2
Cement board sizes

Thickness (inches)	Panel Widths (inches)	Panel Lengths (feet)
½, ⅝	32, 36, 38	5 to 8 standard
		3 to 8 standard

penetration-typically 1⅛ to 1¼ inches for one-hour fire-rated wall assemblies.

Drywall Screws

Drywall screws have greater holding power than nails and are preferred by many contractors. They will have fewer pop-outs—resulting in fewer call-backs for further repairs.

For most purposes, the buglehead screw is used (3–6). It is power driven and produces a uniform, controlled penetration of the panel.

The types available are:

Type-W Used to secure the gypsum panel to wood framing.

Type-S Used to secure the gypsum panel to steel studs. This is a self-drilling, self-tapping fastener.

Type-G Used to secure gypsum panels to gypsum backing or base material. They should be long enough to penetrate the base panel at least ½ inch.

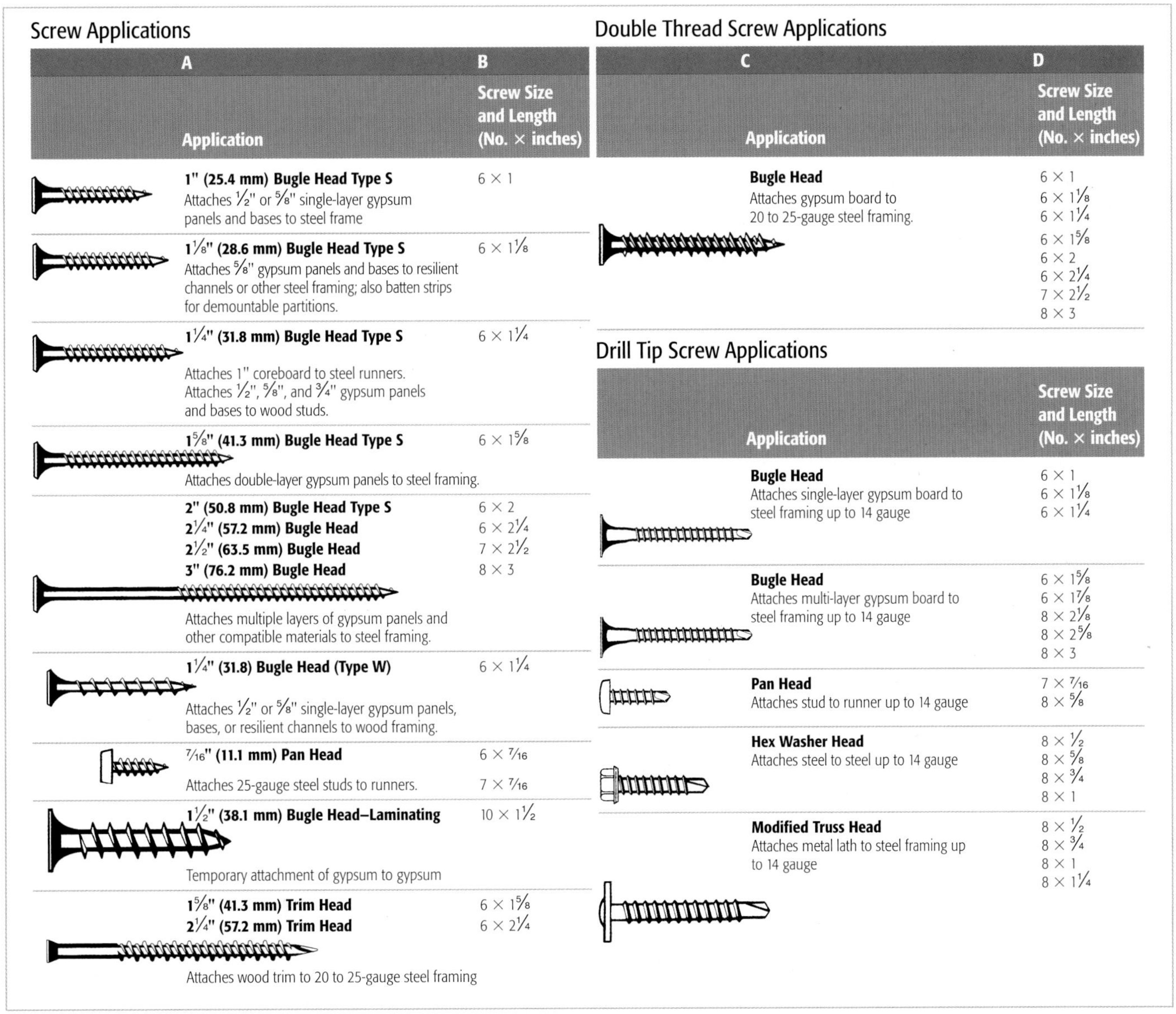

▼ **3–6.** The types of drywall screws used to secure panels to wood and steel framing. Also shown are drill tip screws used to secure steel to steel framing members. (*Courtesy National Gypsum Company*).

Screw Applications

A	B
Application	**Screw Size and Length (No. × inches)**
1" (25.4 mm) Bugle Head Type S Attaches ½" or ⅝" single-layer gypsum panels and bases to steel frame	6 × 1
1⅛" (28.6 mm) Bugle Head Type S Attaches ⅝" gypsum panels and bases to resilient channels or other steel framing; also batten strips for demountable partitions.	6 × 1⅛
1¼" (31.8 mm) Bugle Head Type S Attaches 1" coreboard to steel runners. Attaches ½", ⅝", and ¾" gypsum panels and bases to wood studs.	6 × 1¼
1⅝" (41.3 mm) Bugle Head Type S Attaches double-layer gypsum panels to steel framing.	6 × 1⅝
2" (50.8 mm) Bugle Head Type S **2¼" (57.2 mm) Bugle Head** **2½" (63.5 mm) Bugle Head** **3" (76.2 mm) Bugle Head** Attaches multiple layers of gypsum panels and other compatible materials to steel framing.	6 × 2 6 × 2¼ 7 × 2½ 8 × 3
1¼" (31.8) Bugle Head (Type W) Attaches ½" or ⅝" single-layer gypsum panels, bases, or resilient channels to wood framing.	6 × 1¼
7/16" (11.1 mm) Pan Head Attaches 25-gauge steel studs to runners.	6 × 7/16 7 × 7/16
1½" (38.1 mm) Bugle Head–Laminating Temporary attachment of gypsum to gypsum	10 × 1½
1⅝" (41.3 mm) Trim Head **2¼" (57.2 mm) Trim Head** Attaches wood trim to 20 to 25-gauge steel framing	6 × 1⅝ 6 × 2¼

Double Thread Screw Applications

C	D
Application	**Screw Size and Length (No. × inches)**
Bugle Head Attaches gypsum board to 20 to 25-gauge steel framing.	6 × 1 6 × 1⅛ 6 × 1¼ 6 × 1⅝ 6 × 2 6 × 2¼ 7 × 2½ 8 × 3

Drill Tip Screw Applications

Application	Screw Size and Length (No. × inches)
Bugle Head Attaches single-layer gypsum board to steel framing up to 14 gauge	6 × 1 6 × 1⅛ 6 × 1¼
Bugle Head Attaches multi-layer gypsum board to steel framing up to 14 gauge	6 × 1⅝ 6 × 1⅞ 8 × 2⅛ 8 × 2⅝ 8 × 3
Pan Head Attaches stud to runner up to 14 gauge	7 × 7/16 8 × ⅝
Hex Washer Head Attaches steel to steel up to 14 gauge	8 × ½ 8 × ⅝ 8 × ¾ 8 × 1
Modified Truss Head Attaches metal lath to steel framing up to 14 gauge	8 × ½ 8 × ¾ 8 × 1 8 × 1¼

TABLE 3–3
Fastener sizes for Singer-Layer Installations

Fastener Type	Drywall Thickness (inches)	Minimum Length of Fastener (inches)
Ring shank or cooler nails into wood	$\frac{1}{4}, \frac{3}{8}, \frac{1}{2}, \frac{5}{8}$	$1\frac{1}{4}, 1\frac{3}{8}$
Type-S bugle-head screw into steel	$\frac{1}{2}, \frac{5}{8}, \frac{3}{4}$	$1, 1\frac{1}{4}$
Type-W bugle-head screw into wood	$\frac{3}{8}, \frac{1}{2}, \frac{5}{8}$	$\frac{1}{4}$
Cement board to wood or steel with special galvanized nails or screws	$\frac{1}{2}, \frac{5}{8}$	$1\frac{5}{8}, 2\frac{1}{4}$

FASTENER LENGTH

The length of the fastener varies depending upon the thickness of the gypsum wallboard and whether it is secured to wood or steel framing. Recommendations for single-layer panel installations are in **Table 3–3**. Codes will have additional requirements for multiple layers of wallboard.

Staples

Staples are used to secure gypsum panels to wood studs only when the panels are the base layer in multi-ply construction. They must have at least a $\frac{7}{16}$-inch crown and be made from 16-gauge, flattened, galvanized wire, and have spreading points (**Table 3–4**). They must penetrate the wood framing at least $\frac{5}{8}$ inch.

Adhesives and Sealants

Adhesives and sealants are applied with manual and power-activated caulking and sealing equipment. For small jobs, a cartridge-type hand-operated gun is widely used (**3–7**). It is used to apply adhesive to a stud or the back of a drywall panel cartridge, which is placed in the gun. The nozzle of the cartridge is cut and a wire is forced into the cartridge, cutting the membrane inside

▲ **3–7.** Adhesives are sold in cartridges and extruded by pressure from a plate in the gun. Some use compressed air to force the extrusion.

that seals the adhesive in the cartridge. The angle of the cut and the size of the opening can be varied to suit the situation (**3–8**). As the trigger on the gun is squeezed, a plunger moves into the end of the cartridge, pushing the caulking or adhesive out of the nozzle.

One power-operated gun uses compressed air and has the adhesive or sealant in a cartridge similar to the hand-operated gun (**3–9**). Large, high-production power-operated pumping machines use adhesive or caulking that is purchased in bulk. This provides a high-volume source as is needed on large commercial building construction (**3–10**).

TABLE 3–4
Typical sizes of power-driven staples.

Staple	3/8	1/2	9/16	19/32	5/8	21/32	3/4	7/8	1	1 1/8	1 1/4	1 3/8	1 1/2	1 3/4	2
21 gauge, 3/16 crown									X						
20 gauge, 3/16 crown			X										X		
18 & 19 gauge, 7/32 crown	X				X		X	X	X	X	X	X	X		
16 gauge, 1/2 crown							X	X	X	X	X	X	X	X	X
16 gauge, 1 crown	X			X		X	X	X	X	X	X		X	X	X
15½ gauge, 1/2 crown													X	X	X

All dimensions in inches. X refers to availability of staple in that particular size.

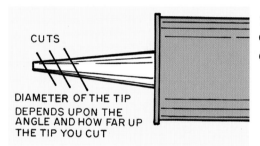

◀ **3–8.** The diameter that you cut the plastic tip on the nozzle of a drywall panel cartridge determines the size of the adhesive extruded.

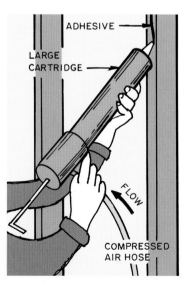

▲ **3–9.** Adhesives can be rapidly placed using a pneumatic-operated gun, which will also place caulking.

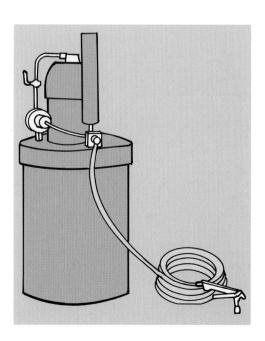

◀ **3–10.** High-production power-operated adhesive and caulking machines provide a large supply of material.

▲ **3–11.** Sealing the bottom plate at the floor with acoustic sealant reduces the flow of noise to adjoining rooms. On exterior walls, it also reduces air flow into and out of the house.

These same guns are used to place sealants. Sealants are used to seal the edges of drywall panels where they meet the floor or another material. This reduces the transfer of noise to the adjoining rooms, so it is part of the acoustical control planned for a building (**3–11**).

Estimating Drywall Materials

4

WHETHER THE JOB IS BIG OR SMALL, *it is necessary to estimate the amount of materials needed. It is better for you to get a little extra and be able to complete the job without having to run back to the building supply dealer for additional items. In addition to a materials estimate, try to make a realistic estimate on the time that will be required to complete the job.*

Commercial installers have to figure material and labor costs so that they can give a firm bid to the general contractor. In addition to relying on their own experience, installers have available a number of commercial estimating publications that give material and labor cost factors.

A Simplified Estimating Plan

The following sections present an approach to a simplified estimating plan that can be used by the person who wants to do a small job, such as a room addition. A brief explanation of the factors that must be considered for large commercial applications completes this chapter.

DETERMINING HOW MUCH WALLBOARD TO USE

For a small job, such as a single room, it is advantageous to decide how you are going to place the panels and the sizes you will use on each wall. Remember, plan as though any openings (doors, windows) are covered. The cut-out material for these is waste.

An exception can be made if there is a large opening such as a picture window or wide door opening between rooms.

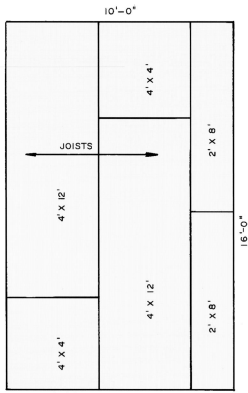

10'-0"

4' X 4'

2' X 8'

JOISTS

4' X 12'

16'-0"

4' X 12'

2' X 8'

4' X 4'

POSSIBLE CEILING LAYOUT
(WOULD BE DIFFERENT IF JOISTS RUN THE
OTHER DIRECTION)
REQUIRES 2- 4' X 12' PANELS
2 - 4' X 8' PANELS

▶ **4–1.** A good ceiling layout uses the longest panels possible and staggers end joints.

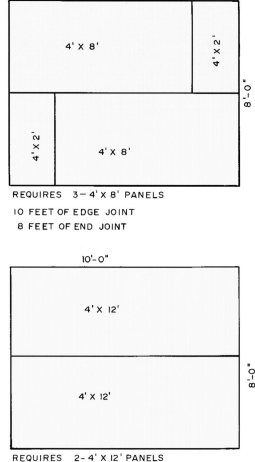

10'-0"

4' X 8'

4' X 2'

4' X 2'

4' X 8'

8'-0"

REQUIRES 3 – 4' X 8' PANELS
10 FEET OF EDGE JOINT
8 FEET OF END JOINT

10'-0"

4' X 12'

4' X 12'

8'-0"

REQUIRES 2 – 4' X 12' PANELS
10 FEET OF EDGE JOINTS
NO END JOINTS

BEST CHOICE

When planning the panel layout, you should consider two main factors-cost and time. Wallboard panels 8 and 12 feet long are widely available. The 12-foot length costs more than the 8-foot length but can cover the wall faster and often eliminates end joints. If you can cover a wall with a 12-foot panel (such as for a 10-foot-long wall) it is faster and costs less than using 8-foot material because of the time saved, especially for taping.

The same technique can be applied to the ceiling. Look at the example room shown in **4–1.** This room is 10 × 16 feet. The ceiling layout will require two 12-foot panels and two 8-foot panels. This permits the end butt joints to be staggered and at least 4 feet apart. End butt joints should never line up.

▲ **4–2.** Two possibilities for a short wall: it is best covered with long panels, even though some drywall is cut off and wasted. The loss due to waste is small. The savings for not having to tape two end joints is large.

A layout for a 10-foot wall is shown in **4–2.** Two possibilities are given. The one using 12-foot panels is the best because it has no end joints. The amount of waste caused by cutting off the end of the panel is negligible. To find the number of panels, simply count them for the ceiling and each wall.

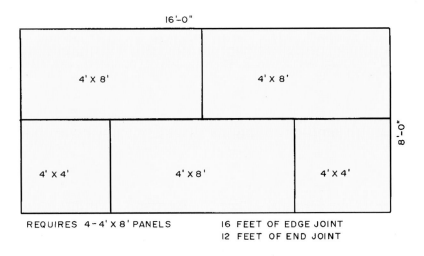

REQUIRES 4-4' X 8' PANELS   16 FEET OF EDGE JOINT
12 FEET OF END JOINT

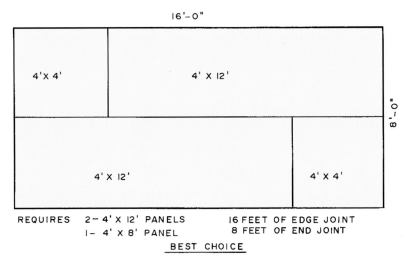

REQUIRES   2 - 4' X 12' PANELS   16 FEET OF EDGE JOINT
1 - 4' X 8' PANEL   8 FEET OF END JOINT
BEST CHOICE

▲ **4-3.** Two possible panel layouts for a medium-long wall. Notice that the use of longer panels eliminates one end joint.

A layout for a 16-foot wall is shown in 4–3. Again, two possible arrangements are shown. The one using 12-foot panels has fewer feet of end butt joints, and would be preferable even if the cost for the panels is greater. Taping is difficult, time-consuming, and costly because of the labor charges.

I suggest you make a wall and ceiling layout as I did in illustrating these points. It only takes a few minutes and is well worth the time.

ESTIMATING THE NUMBER OF NAILS

A simple way to do this for a small job is to use the nail count per panel. These numbers are in **Tables 4–1** and **4–2**. Multiply the number of nails in each size panel by the number of panels. If you figure there are about 300 nails per pound, you can divide the total number of nails needed by 300 to get a close estimate of how many pounds of nails you will need. I suggest buying six pounds.

TABLE 4-1
Number of Nails Needed per Panel (for panels installed horizontally)

| | Number of Nails per Panel | |
	Single-Nailed	Double-Nailed
4' x 8' panel	49	64
4' x 12' panel	63	70
(Number of nails per pound approx. 300)		

TABLE 4-2
Total Number of Nails Needed

	No. of Panels	Nails per Panel	Total Nails
4' x 8' panels	20	49	980
4' x 12' panels	10	63	630
		Nails Needed	1,610
Approximately 300 nails per pound		Buy 6 pounds of nails	

When installing single-layer wallboard with ring-shank nails, the nails are typically spaced 8 inches O.C. in the field and on the edges of panels over studs 16 inches O.C. For ceiling installations, nails are typically spaced 7 inches O.C. in the field and on the edges with joists spaced 16 inches O.C. See Chapter 5 for double-layer panels.

ESTIMATING THE NUMBER OF SCREWS

Screws are typically placed 16 inches O.C. on the edges and interiors of wall panels and 12 inches O.C. on the edges and interiors of ceilings. Requirements for several panel sizes are given in **Table 4–3**.

DETERMINING HOW MUCH TAPE TO USE

Since you now know the placement of the gypsum wallboard panels, you can add up the number of lineal feet of tape required for each wall and the ceiling. Tape is usually available in 100-foot rolls. Another way is to figure about 380 lineal feet of tape per 1000 square feet of drywall.

DETERMINING HOW MANY CORNER BEADS TO USE

Corner beads are made in 8-foot lengths, so buy one for each outside corner. Do not plan to use short pieces because they create an end butt joint, which is difficult to get flat and cover with tape and joint compound.

DETERMINING HOW MUCH JOINT COMPOUND TO USE

Joint compound is sold in containers specified in gallons and in pounds. The amount required per 1,000 square feet of drywall varies for different types of compound. To accurately estimate the amount needed, it is necessary to review the manufacturer's recommendations. In **Table 4–4**, typical coverage requirements are listed for several types of joint compounds.

DETERMINING HOW MUCH ADHESIVE TO USE

Adhesive is sold in both cartridges that contain a specified number of ounces and in gallon containers. Typical coverage figures are shown in **Table 4–5**.

TABLE 4–3
Number of Screws Needed for Ceilings

	Number of Screws per Panel Ceiling, 12" O.C.	Walls, 16" O.C.
4' x 8' panel	35	28
4' x 12' panel	50	37

TABLE 4–4
Typical Joint Compound Coverages

Compounds	Required per 1,000 Square Feet
Standard all-purpose premixed	150 pounds
Lightweight all-purpose	67 pounds
Powdered	85 pounds
Setting-type	75 pounds
Texturing	240 pounds

TABLE 4–5
Typical Adhesive Coverage

Coverage		$\frac{1}{4}$-inch-diameter Bead	$\frac{3}{8}$-inch-diameter Bead
100 lineal feet	gallons	2½ gallons	5 gallons
	30 oz. cartridges	11 cartridges	26 cartridges

Ceiling	20 x 15	=	300 SQ. FT.	
Walls	(20+15+20+15) x 8	=	560 SQ. FT.	
Total		=	860 SQ. FT	of drywall SURFACE
No. of 4' x 8' panels		=	860 x 0.03125	= 26.9 (order 28)
Pounds of 1⅜" nails		=	860 x 0.0050	= 4.3 (order 5 lbs.)
Tubes of adhesives		=	860 x 0.0020	= 1.7 (order 2)
Rolls of tape		=	860 x 0.00167	= 1.4 (order 2)
Five-gallon joint-compound buckets		=	860 x 0.00100	= 0.9 (order 1)

Estimating Drywall Materials for a Commercial Job

The following information gives a brief look at what a commercial drywall installer might do to prepare a bid and figure the materials to order for delivery to a job.

To estimate the amount of materials needed on a large job, calculate the area of the ceilings and walls in all the rooms, halls, closets, garages, and other spaces to be covered. To do this, find the length of each wall and add them together to get the perimeter length. (These distances can be found on the architectural drawings.) Multiply the perimeter by the wall height to get the **square feet of wall area.** Multiply the length by the width of the ceiling to get the **square feet of the ceiling.** An example is given in **4–4.**

Follow this estimating procedure for each area to be covered. Do not allow for wall openings. To find the number of panels needed—and the amount of tape, joint compound, and nails that will be required—multiply the total square feet by the estimating factors presented in **Table 4–6.** For example, if the total square feet of area to be covered is 368 square feet, the number of 4' × 8' panels would be 368 × 0.03130, which equals 11.5 or 12 panels.

To estimate the number of hours required for installing and finishing drywall, various companies supply extensive tables giving standardized times for performing various tasks. A brief abstract of part of one of these tables is in **Table 4–7.** It gives the estimated minimum time, average time, and maximum time factors.

Table 4–8 provides a way to estimate the labor hours required to install and finish a room. Once you get the total hours, multiply it by the hourly rates to get the total cost of the job.

▲ **4–4.** An example of estimating the materials needed for a room. This example uses 4 ft. x 8 ft. panels. Figure a better layout and panel size and refigure the quantities.

TABLE 4–6
Factors for the Installation and Finishing of Gypsum Wallboard

Material	Factor	Gives
4' x 8' panel	0.03130	No. of panels
4' x 12' panel	0.02087	No. of panels
1⅜" annual ring nails (single-nailed)	0.0054	Pounds of nails
Adhesive	0.00209	Tubes of adhesive
Tape	0.00170	No. of rolls
Joint compound	0.00105	No. of five-gallon cans
Joint compound (for textured ceiling)	0.00255	No. of five-gallon cans

(Reproduced with permission from *Carpentry Estimating,* by W.P. Jackson, Craftsman Book Company, 6058 Corte del Cedro, Carlsbad, CA 92009)

TABLE 4–7
Man-hour Estimating Factors* for Drywall Nailed or Screwed to Wood Framing

Activity	Man-hours per square foot	
½″ drywall		
	ceiling	0.009
	walls	0.008
Taping & finishing		
	minimum	0.006
	average	0.008
	maximum	0.009
Man-hours per linear foot		
Installing corner bead		
	minimum	0.025
	average	0.029
	maximum	0.042

* These are for illustration purposes only. Contact an estimating organization for accurate figures for your area.
(Reproduced with permission from the 1995 *General Construction Costbook,* Building News, 3055 Overland Ave., Los Angeles, CA 90034)

TABLE 4–8
Man-hour Installation and Finishing Estimates

Installing 1/2″ wallboard			
Ceiling	300 sq.ft x 0.009.	=	2.7 hours
Walls	560 sq.ft. x 0.008	=	4.5 hours
Taping and finishing	860 sq. ft. x 0.008	=	6.9 hours
Total			14.1 hours

(Reproduced with permission from the 1995 *General Construction Costbook,* Building News, 3055 Overland Ave., Los Angeles, CA 90034)

Installing Gypsum Wallboard PART II

Installation Skills and Techniques

5

DRYWALL PANELS *must be measured, cut, pierced, and drilled, and then nailed, screwed, or bonded to framing with an adhesive. Both wood and metal framing could be involved. The following material will describe how to work with the gypsum panels as you install them to the framing.*

Measuring

Accurate measuring of the framing to receive the panel, as well as accurate measuring and marking of the panel for cutting, is critical. The old saying "Measure twice, cut once" certainly applies here.

Measuring the framing will reveal if it is out of line or not square. If it is not possible to cut the panel to compensate for this, the framing must be corrected (Refer to Chapter 9 for correcting techniques.) All markings on drywall panels should be made with a soft lead pencil. Do not use a ballpoint pen because if any of the ink shows on the wall after hanging, it will bleed through the joint compound and latex paint. It will sometimes even show through a layer of joint cement.

Chalk lines can be used to mark long cuts. Locate each end of the line on the mark, rub chalk on the line, then lift it slightly and let it snap against the surface. The line must be very tight and lifted straight up a very small amount. Long wood and metal straightedges will also work.

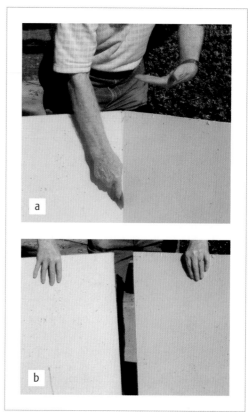

▲ **5–3.** After the core has snapped, cut the back paper, separating the panel into two pieces.

▲ **5–1.** Place the drywall T-square against the panel and score the face paper and the gypsum core with a sharp utility knife, cutting from the top down. Notice how the T-square is held in place by the knee and the foot at the floor.

▲ **5–2.** After scoring the face side of the panel, bend it, snapping the core.

▲ **5–4.** If the core is a bit irregular, it can be made smoother with a rasp or surface-forming tool.

INSTALLATION SKILLS AND TECHNIQUES

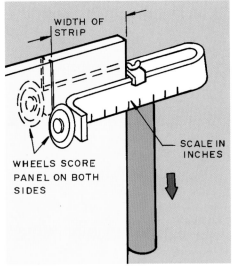

▲ **5-5.** Narrow strips can be cut using a drywall stripper, which scores both sides of the panel. It will cut strips up to 4½ inches wide.

▲ **5-6.** Long cuts can be made using a steel tape measure that has a guide to slide along the edge of the panel and a slot in the end to hold the utility knife blade.

Cutting Drywall Panels

Panels are usually cut using a utility knife. Most prefer to cut the face side first so a sharp, clean edge is produced. While you can cut from the back first, it is more difficult to get a straight, clean cut edge on the face paper with the second cut.

To cut a panel across the width, measure and mark the location. Then place the drywall T-square against the panel and score the gypsum core with a utility knife (5-1). Then bend the panel, causing the core to snap (5-2). Next, run the utility knife down the channel that formed as the panel was snapped, and separate the panel (5-3). If the edge of the core is irregular (causing possible problems if it butts another panel), it can be smoothed with a rasp or surface-forming tool (5-4).

Remember to replace the blade in the utility knife frequently. It must always be very sharp.

Long narrow pieces can be cut using a drywall stripper. It scores both sides in a single pass. Then snap off the piece (5-5). Typically, long horizontal cuts are made by running a steel measuring tape that has an adjustable edge guide and a tip that holds the utility knife blade. Place the edge guide on the edge of the panel, place the knife blade into the slot, and move both hands together, drawing the tool down the full length of the panel. Bend to snap the panel and make the back cut freehand (5-6).

CUTTING SMALL OPENINGS IN DRYWALL PANELS

There are several techniques commonly used to locate and cut small openings, such as an electric box, in the drywall. One technique is to mark the location of the sides of the box on the floor with a framing square. Measure and mark the height of the top of the box on the floor

▶ **5–7.** Locate the position of the box on the subfloor and write its height there also.

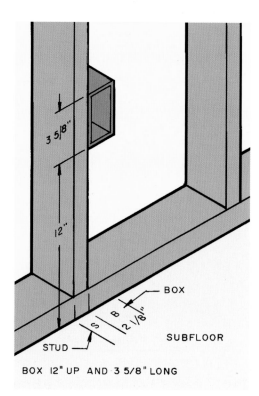

3 5/8"

12"

BOX

B
2 1/8"

S

STUD

SUBFLOOR

BOX 12" UP AND 3 5/8" LONG

(5–7). Now install the drywall on the wall and measure up and mark the outline of the box on it (5–8). Cut to the outside edge of the box with a drywall keyhole saw or utility knife (5–9). Cut as close to the edges of the box as possible. If a wide gap occurs, air can infiltrate into the house. Generally, any gap is filled with caulking. It is easier to cut round holes with a utility knife.

The cuts can be made using an electric drywall router instead of a saw. It works fast and produces a smooth cut (5–10). The router bit should not be more than ¼ inch longer than the thickness of the panel. If the wiring is already in the box, you will have to tuck it in tight so the router bit does not hit. Start the router and insert it inside the marked outline. Move it carefully to the side until it touches the side of the box. Raise it enough so it moves to the outside of the

▶ **5–8.** Lightly tack the drywall panel over the box. Use a framing square to locate the sides on the panel.

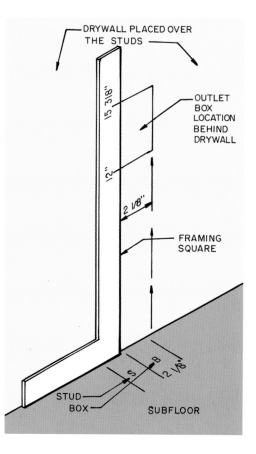

DRYWALL PLACED OVER THE STUDS

15 3/8"

OUTLET BOX LOCATION BEHIND DRYWALL

12"

2 1/8"

FRAMING SQUARE

2 1/8"

B

S

STUD

BOX

SUBFLOOR

▲ **5–9.** You can cut out the box opening with a utility knife or drywall keyhole saw. *(Courtesy The Stanley Works)*

▶ **5–10.** When cutting an opening with a router, insert the cutter inside the marked area to be removed. Then move it until it touches the side of the box, lift it over the side, and plunge it into the panel. Then cut around the outside perimeter of the box. *(Courtesy Bosch Tool Corporation)*

box and proceed to cut around the perimeter. The router is a very versatile tool for making other cuts in drywall. Wear a dust mask when using it.

Another technique is to use a commercially available electric box cutout locator. It is a template that clips to the box. The gypsum panel is set in place and pressed against the locator, which has an adhesive face. It sticks to the panel and you trace around it, thus locating the cuts for the box (5–11 and 5–12). The template can be reused many times.

Round holes can be cut with the drywall circle cutter shown in Chapter 2.

First, locate the center of the circle. This is typically a round electric box in the ceiling used for installing a light. Then drive a nail through the panel at the center before the panel is installed. Put the pin of the circle cutter in the hole and rotate the cutting end, scoring the drywall. Then, repeat on the back side of the panel. Next, knock out the plug from the front side of the panel (5–13). If necessary, smooth irregularities around the edge so it fits around the outlet.

Circular holes can also be cut with a keyhole saw. Locate and mark the circumference of the hole. The saw has a

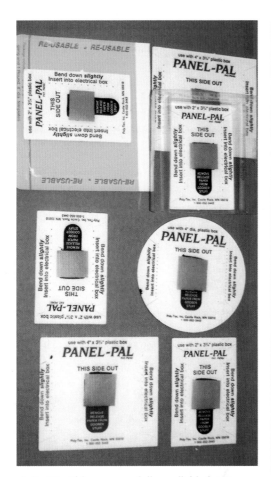

▲ **5–11.** This commercially available locator template kit provides templates for four single-gang, two double-gang, and one round, 4-inch-diameter box.

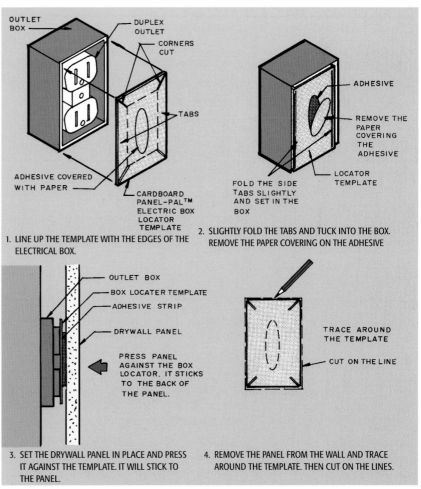

1. LINE UP THE TEMPLATE WITH THE EDGES OF THE ELECTRICAL BOX.

2. SLIGHTLY FOLD THE TABS AND TUCK INTO THE BOX. REMOVE THE PAPER COVERING ON THE ADHESIVE

3. SET THE DRYWALL PANEL IN PLACE AND PRESS IT AGAINST THE TEMPLATE. IT WILL STICK TO THE PANEL.

4. REMOVE THE PANEL FROM THE WALL AND TRACE AROUND THE TEMPLATE. THEN CUT ON THE LINES.

▲ **5–12.** The use of locator templates lets you quickly locate electrical outlets without measuring. *(Courtesy Poly-Tex, Inc.)*

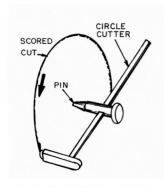

1. AFTER LOCATING THE CENTER OF THE HOLE, DRIVE A SMALL NAIL THROUGH THE PANEL. THEN INSERT THE PIN IN THE LEG OF THE CIRCLE CUTTER IN THE HOLE AND SCORE THE PANEL ON ONE FACE. REPEAT ON THE BACK.

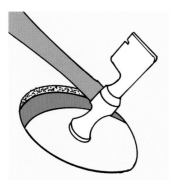

2. AFTER THE PANEL HAS BEEN DEEPLY SCORED ON BOTH SIDES, TAPE OUT THE PLUG FROM THE FACE SIDE.

▲ **5–13.** Circular openings can be cut with a drywall circle cutter. Score both sides of the panel and knock out the plug. This is done before the panel is mounted on the wall.

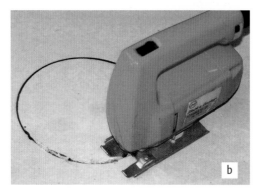

▲ **5–14.** Circles and other shaped openings can be cut with a keyhole saw or electric saber saw.

sharp tip that is placed against the drywall and rotated, drilling a hole through it. The teeth of the saw then hit the core and cut along the line, marking the hole (**5–14**). If the saw does not have a cutting tip, you will have to drill a hole through the panel, insert the saw in it, and make the cut.

A power **saber saw** can be used instead of the keyhole saw. The end of the blade will cut through the panel if you tilt the saw and slowly lower it into the panel. This is called plunge cutting (**5–15**).

Holes can be cut by scoring the outline with a knife and cutting across the diagonals (**5–16**). Then tap out the pieces and cut the back paper, smoothing up the core on the back. Always mark and cut from the finish side of the panel.

All types of openings can also be cut with a drywall router, which has a special bit. This is shown in **5–10**.

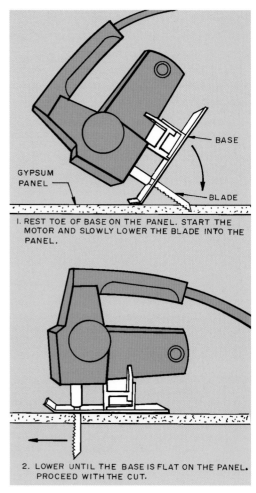

1. REST TOE OF BASE ON THE PANEL. START THE MOTOR AND SLOWLY LOWER THE BLADE INTO THE PANEL.

2. LOWER UNTIL THE BASE IS FLAT ON THE PANEL. PROCEED WITH THE CUT.

▲ **5–15.** A saber saw can plunge-cut a hole in the gypsum panel and cut openings of any shape.

A tool designed to penetrate and cut holes in gypsum, plywood, reconstituted wood panels, plastic panels, aluminum, ceramic tile, and plaster is shown in **5–17**. It uses a special Spiracut Bit that will plunge through the drywall and make clean cuts as it is being moved clockwise around the marked opening.

Rectangular holes can also be cut using the keyhole saw or electric saber saw. Use the same procedure as described for circular holes (refer to **5–9** and **5–10**).

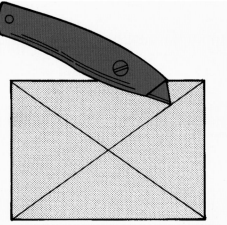

1. DEEPLY SCORE THE EDGES AND DIAGONALS

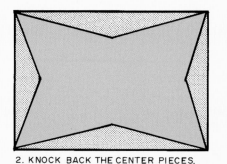

2. KNOCK BACK THE CENTER PIECES, CUT THE BACK PAPER. SMOOTH THE EDGES.

▲ **5-16.** Holes can be cut with a utility knife by scoring the edges and cutting across diagonals. Then knock back the pieces and trim the paper on the back.

Fastener Sizes

Gypsum wallboard is secured to wood framing with nails, screws, or staples. The accepted types are shown in Chapter 3. Panels that serve as the underlayment for a multilayer installation can be secured

◀ **5-17.** This power tool will plunge through the drywall and cut the opening with a special bit. *(Courtesy Rotozip Tool, Bosch Power Tools and Accessories)*

with nails, screws, or staples. Panels secured to lightweight steel framing are secured with screws. The fasteners must meet the standards set by the American Society for Testing and Materials (ASTM).

Recommended fastener sizes and penetration are shown in **Tables 5–1** to **5–3**. These are specified in the International Residential Code for One- and Two-Family Dwellings, sponsored by the International Code Council (Country Club Hills, Illinois).

The typical spacing for nails, screws, and staples is shown in **Tables 5–4** and **5–5**.

Attaching Panels with Nails

The nail must be set so it holds the panel firmly to the stud, and the head should be set slightly below the surface in a small dimple. The paper facing should not be broken (**5–18**). This provides a space for the joint compound to conceal the nail. The face of the hammer is curved to form this dimple. Power nailers can be

TABLE 5–1
Minimum Nail Lengths with and without adhesive

NAIL TYPES			
Wallboard thickness	**Annular ring**	**Cooler**	**Gypsum Board**
⅜ inch	1¼ inches	1⅜ inches	
½ inch	1⅜ inches	1⅜ inches	1⅜ inches
⅝ inch	1⅝ inches	1⅞ inches	1⅞ inches

Data taken with permission from Table R702.3.5, International Residential Code for One- and Two-Family Dwellings, International Code Council, Inc.

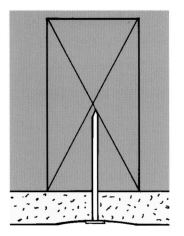

▲ 5–18. The nail head is set in a slight dimple so it can be covered with joint compound.

TABLE 5–2
Minimum Screw Lengths

Application	Type	Drywall Thickness	Minimum Fastener Length	Minimum Penetration
Wood Framing	W	⅜ inch	1 inch	
	Or	½ inch	1⅛ inches	⅝ inch
	S	⅝ inch	1¼ inches	
Light Gauge Steel	S	⅜ inch	¾ inch	
		½ inch	⅞ inch	⅜ inch
		⅝ inch	1 inch	

Data taken with permission from Table R702.3.5, International Residential Code for One- and Two-Family Dwellings, International Code Council, Inc.

TABLE 5–3
Minimum Staple Lengths

Wallboard Thickness	Length	Minimum Penetration
⅜"	1"	⅝"
½"	1⅛"	⅝"
⅝"	1¼"	⅝"

Data taken with permission from Table R702.3.5, International Residential Code for One- and Two-Family Dwellings, International Code Council, Inc.

TABLE 5–4
Fastener Spacing, Single Application without Adhesive

Fastener	Location	Framing Spacing 16 inches O.C.	Framing Spacing 24 inches O.C.
Nails	Ceilings	7 inches	7 inches
	Walls	8 inches	8 inches
Screws	Ceilings	12 inches	12 inches
	Walls	16 inches	12 inches
Staples	Ceilings	7 inches	7 inches
	Walls	7 inches	7 inches

TABLE 5–5
Fastener Spacing, Single Application with Adhesive

Fastener	Location	Framing Spacing 16 inches O.C.	Framing Spacing 24 inches O.C.
Nails	Ceilings	16 inches	16 inches
	Walls	16 inches	16 inches
Screws	Ceilings	16 inches	16 inches
	Walls	16 inches	24 inches
Staples	Ceilings	16 inches	16 inches
	Walls	16 inches	16 inches

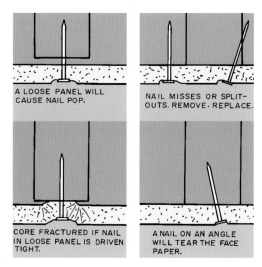

A LOOSE PANEL WILL CAUSE NAIL POP.

NAIL MISSES OR SPLIT-OUTS. REMOVE · REPLACE.

CORE FRACTURED IF NAIL IN LOOSE PANEL IS DRIVEN TIGHT.

A NAIL ON AN ANGLE WILL TEAR THE FACE PAPER.

▲ **5–19.** Examples of improper nailing that will eventually lead to nail pops and panel damage.

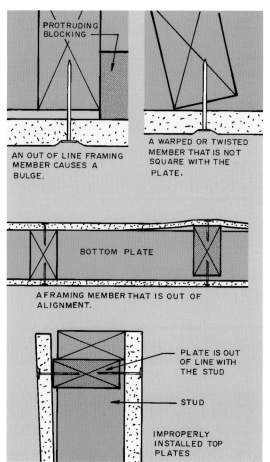

PROTRUDING BLOCKING

AN OUT OF LINE FRAMING MEMBER CAUSES A BULGE.

A WARPED OR TWISTED MEMBER THAT IS NOT SQUARE WITH THE PLATE.

BOTTOM PLATE

A FRAMING MEMBER THAT IS OUT OF ALIGNMENT.

PLATE IS OUT OF LINE WITH THE STUD

STUD

IMPROPERLY INSTALLED TOP PLATES

▲ **5–20.** Defective framing will cause damage to the panel surface over time.

adjusted so they have only enough of a blow to seat the nail, produce a dimple, but not tear the paper or break the gypsum core.

Improper nailing is probably the main cause for nail pops and other problems that emerge after the job is finished. Among these are nails that are not set in enough to hold the panel to the stud; a nail that misses the stud; a nail driven when the panel was not tight against the stud (rupturing the core); and nails driven on an angle, which break the face paper (**5–19**). In addition, twisted or warped studs, studs out of line, and inadequate backing cause problems in the future (**5–20**). Remove any nails that are improperly driven.

NAILING PATTERNS

Gypsum panels can be either single-nailed or double-nailed. Double-nailing produces a better job. In some cases, as in a fire wall, building codes specify double-nailing. The use of annular-ring nails also improves the installation.

Single-nailed patterns are shown in 5–21 and double-nailed patterns are shown in 5–22.

▼ **5–21.** The nails on single-nailed gypsum panels are spaced 7 to 8 inches apart in the field and along the edges. They are not less than ⅜ inch in from the edges and ends of the panels. Nail in the field first and work toward the edges.

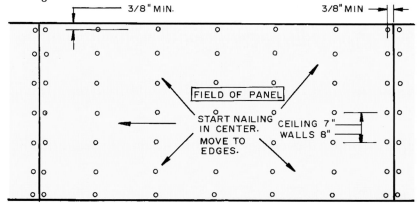

3/8" MIN.

3/8" MIN.

FIELD OF PANEL

START NAILING IN CENTER. MOVE TO EDGES.

CEILING 7" WALLS 8"

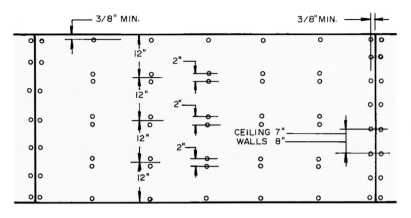

▲ **5–22.** To double-nail a panel, first drive one set of nails in the field and on the ends and edges of the panel. Then go back and place a second series of nails spaced 2 inches from those in the field.

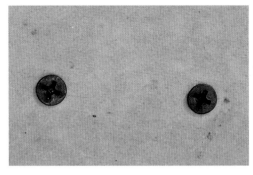

▲ **5–23.** Double nailing or screwing minimizes the possibility of nail-pop.

Following are recommended procedures to follow for nailing gypsum panels.

1. Begin nailing from the edge of the panel that butts one already in place. Nail all nails on each stud (perimeter and/or those in the field of the panel) as you move across the panel. *DO NOT nail the perimeter first and then nail the field.*
2. Locate the nails on butting edges or ends opposite each other.
3. Drive the nails at least ⅜ inch in from the ends and edges of the panel.
4. Press the panel hard against the stud before setting the nail.
5. Keep the shank of the nail perpendicular to the panel.
6. Set the head of the nail in a shallow dimple, but do not break the face paper or crush the gypsum core.
7. Space nails on the perimeter 7 inches O.C. on ceilings and 8 inches O.C. for walls, and 12 inches O.C. in the field. Ceilings should be double-nailed. You should note that double nailing minimizes nail-pop (**5–23**).

Attaching Panels with Staples

Staples are used only to attach the base layer panels to wood framing when a double-layer construction is to be used. Staples are placed with the crown perpendicular to the gypsum board edges except where the edges fall on supports. Here, they are installed parallel to the edge of the panel (**5–24**).

Adjust the stapler so that the staples yield a shallow dimple as shown in **5–25**. They should not cut through the face paper and go into the gypsum core. Staples are spaced 7 inches O.C. on ceilings and on sidewalls, and ⅜ inch from the edges of the panel.

Attaching Panels with Screws

Screws are used to attach panels to wood and metal studs. You can find information on screws and screw guns in Chapters 2 and 3. They are installed with an electric screw gun that has a magnetic chuck and an adjustable screw-depth control. The screw head should be slightly below the surface of the panel (**5–26**). Be certain to drive the screw perpendicular to the face of the panel and firmly into the stud. If it misses the stud or is on an angle, it should be removed and another should be properly driven.

Install the screws as described for nails by beginning on the end that butts another panel and working across the panel, installing perimeter and field screws as you go. Recommended placement for a single-screw application is shown in **5–27**. On ceilings, you should space screws not more than 12 inches

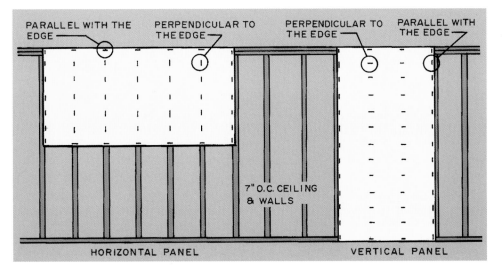

PARALLEL WITH THE EDGE — PERPENDICULAR TO THE EDGE — PERPENDICULAR TO THE EDGE — PARALLEL WITH THE EDGE

7" O.C. CEILING & WALLS

HORIZONTAL PANEL   VERTICAL PANEL

◄ **5–24.** Staples are installed with the crown parallel to the edge of the panel.

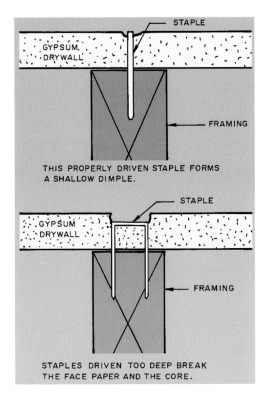

STAPLE

GYPSUM DRYWALL

FRAMING

THIS PROPERLY DRIVEN STAPLE FORMS A SHALLOW DIMPLE.

STAPLE

GYPSUM DRYWALL

FRAMING

STAPLES DRIVEN TOO DEEP BREAK THE FACE PAPER AND THE CORE.

▲ **5–25.** Properly driven staples form a slight dimple and do not break the paper.

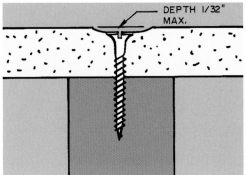

DEPTH 1/32" MAX.

◄ **5–26.** The proper depth to drive a screw.

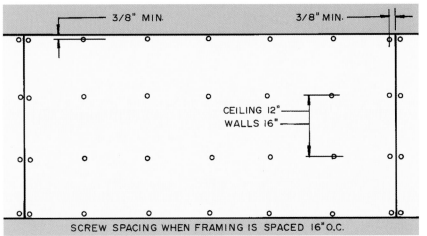

3/8" MIN.   3/8" MIN.

CEILING 12"
WALLS 16"

SCREW SPACING WHEN FRAMING IS SPACED 16" O.C.

▲ **5–27.** When single-screw applications are used to mechanically attach a single layer of gypsum board to wood framing spaced 16 inches O.C., the screws are spaced 12 inches O.C. on the ceiling, and 16 O.C. on the wall.

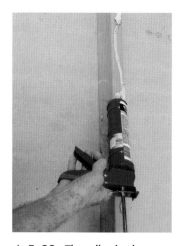

▲ **5–28.** The adhesive is applied to the studs from the cartridge held in a caulking gun.

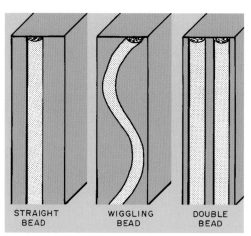

STRAIGHT BEAD   WIGGLING BEAD   DOUBLE BEAD

▲ **5–29.** Methods for applying adhesives to studs.

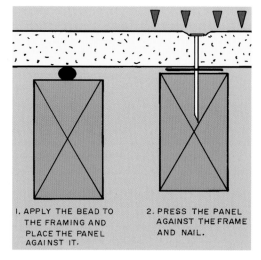

1. APPLY THE BEAD TO THE FRAMING AND PLACE THE PANEL AGAINST IT.

2. PRESS THE PANEL AGAINST THE FRAME AND NAIL.

▲ **5–30.** Press the panel firmly against the stud so the adhesive spreads out in a thin layer.

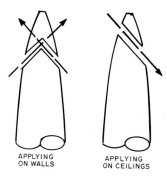

APPLYING ON WALLS   APPLYING ON CEILINGS

▲ **5–31.** The cut on the tip of the cartridge varies depending upon where the adhesive is to be placed.

It helps bond the panel to the studs, reducing nail pops. The use of an adhesive will reduce the number of nails or screws required. (See **Table 5–5**, on page 42.)

Adhesives must be applied directly to the framing members. Sometimes the Kraft paper facing on insulation blankets is stapled over the face of the framing or it is covered with a plastic vapor barrier. Adhesive cannot be applied to these surfaces.

Adhesive is applied to the studs from a cartridge that is placed in a caulking gun as shown in **5–28.** The adhesive is applied in a continuous ⅜-inch bead in the center of the framing in the field of the panel. When two panels butt on a member, two beads can be laid, although some prefer to lay a wiggling bead as shown in **5–29.** When the panel is pressed against the framing and nailed or screwed, the adhesive spreads out, covering most of the face of the framing (**5–30**).

The nozzle on the cartridge is cut in one of two ways, depending upon where the adhesive is to be used (**5–31**). For wall panels, it is cut in a V shape, and for ceiling joists, an angle cut is made. The location of the cut up the tip determines the size of the adhesive extruded.

Make sure you read the directions on the adhesive cartridge before you buy it to be certain it can be used for drywall installation. Do not apply to surfaces that are dirty or have oil or other contaminating materials. In cold weather, keep the room heated above 50°F (10°C) and in the summer do not use if the room temperature exceeds 100°F (38°C). Observe the open time (time it is in place before a panel is applied) on the cartridge so that it has not started to set before the panel is applied. Do not tape the joint for 48 hours after application. Remember, adhesives are flammable, so be cautious about fire and provide adequate ventilation in the room.

O.C., and 16 inches O.C. on walls when the framing is 16 inches O.C. If the framing is 24 inches O.C., space the screws not more than 12 inches O.C. on ceiling and walls.

Attaching Panels with Adhesive

Adhesives are applied to the stud in addition to nailing or fastening with screws.

Double-Layer Applications

Double-layer applications consist of one layer of gypsum drywall nailed or screwed directly to the studs, with a second panel installed over the first layer. The second layer is bonded to the first with an adhesive.

When doing a double-layer application, the adhesive used is a laminating adhesive. This is different from that used to bond panels to wood framing. As you plan the lamination, cut the first face panel so the edge joints do not line directly up with those on the base panels. Some people lay the face panels perpendicular to the base panels.

One laminating technique is to apply the adhesive over the entire back of the face panel using a notched spreader (5–32). This is referred to as **sheet lamination**. The notches in the spreader should be at least ¼ × ¼ inch and spread apart 2 inches O.C. Spreaders with larger notches are available.

Another technique is to apply strips of adhesive on each edge of the panel and one down the center. A special laminating spreader is used for this process (5–33). This is referred to as **strip lamination**, which is sometimes called for in the job specifications. Some jobs specify the use of a liquid contact adhesive. It is applied to both surfaces to be joined with a roller that has a short nap. After both surfaces are dry, they are pressed together, forming the bond. Once they touch, they cannot be moved, so the placement must be precise.

Opinions differ on how to install nails or screws after the face panel is pressed against the base panel. Typically, on wall panels, the fasteners are installed on the top and bottom edges, spaced

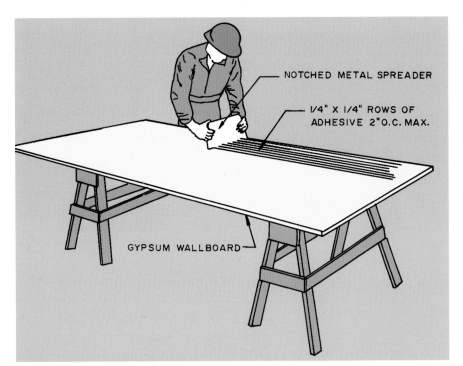

NOTCHED METAL SPREADER

1/4" X 1/4" ROWS OF ADHESIVE 2" O.C. MAX.

GYPSUM WALLBOARD

▲ **5–32.** Double-layer panel application requires the use of an adhesive that is applied to the back of the top panel.

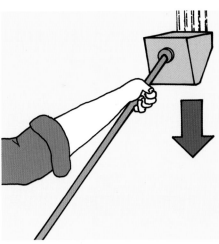

▲ **5–33.** A special applicator is used to apply adhesive on the base panel if it has been secured to the studs.

▲ **5–35.** Locate the opening on the front and back of the panel. Tap a nail through the center of the front. This helps locate the opening on the back of the panel.

▲ **5–34.** After scoring the core on the face side and tapping the cut with a hammer, bend the panel, breaking the core. Then cut the fiberglass mesh on the back side.

24 inches O.C., and pressure is applied in the center of the panel until the adhesive cures. This can be done by installing double-headed scaffold nails into the studs. They are easily removed after the adhesive has set. Laminated ceiling panels are usually fastened along the ends and edges with the fasteners spaced 16 inches O.C. One fastener is installed into each joist in the middle of the panel.

Installing Cement Board

When cutting cement board, wear your safety glasses. Some people prefer to wear gloves. Cement board has an aggregated Portland cement core reinforced on both sides with a fiberglass mesh. While it is very hard, it is cut much the same as standard gypsum wallboard. To make straight cuts, mark the line of cut or use a drywall T-square and cut along the edge

▲ **5–36.** Using a utility knife, cut the fiberglass mesh and score the core on both sides. Some people use a chisel to score the core after cutting the fiberglass mesh.

▲ **5–37.** Carefully tap along the edges of the opening on the face side until the cutout cracks and drops out the back. Rough edges can be trimmed with a coarse file.

▲ **5–38.** If the piece in the opening will not easily drop out, try cutting around the edges with a small hacksaw.

with a utility knife. Since this quickly dulls the blade, some people prefer to use a knife with a carbide-tipped blade. Cut through the mesh facing and score the core. Apply pressure on the back of the panel and tap along the line of cut with a hammer. This will crack the core. Then push the sides forward and cut the mesh on the back (5–34).

Openings can be cut through cement board by locating it on the mesh on one side. Punch a hole through the panel at the center of the opening (5–35). From this point, mark the outline of the opening on the back side of the panel. Cut through the mesh into the cement core on both sides (5–36). Carefully tap the piece to be removed (5–37). It will

break loose and fall out. If it does not move easily, recut the perimeter of the opening. Try to keep from breaking off pieces around the edge of the opening. In difficult cases, striking the edge with a small metal chisel might help, or else forcing a small metal hacksaw blade into an opening and sawing along the perimeter. However, this will quickly dull the blade (5–38).

The cement board is installed with the smooth face out if ceramic tile is to be applied. The studs should not be spaced wider than 16 inches O.C.

Cement board is attached using special galvanized screws or galvanized roofing nails. Most installers also bond the panels to the studs with adhesive.

6 Gypsum Wallboard Installation

HANGING GYPSUM WALLBOARD *is a hard job. It requires lifting heavy panels and holding them in place while they are secured to the framing. It must be done correctly or the finishing operations will be more difficult and problems can occur years after the job is finished. It involves planning, measuring, cutting, placing, and fastening.*

Before You Start to Work

Before installing the gypsum wallboard you should check the framing to see if any corrections are needed. The ceiling joists may not be on the same plane or some studs may be bowed or out of line. The carpenters may have failed to install needed nailing blocks on the top of the wall framing or where walls meet. All corrections should be made before starting to install the drywall.

This chapter is concerned with the placement and installation of the panels of wallboard. Specific techniques—such as cutting and fastening panels—can be found in Chapter 5.

Installation Guidelines

1. Install the gypsum wallboard to the walls after the ceilings have been covered.
2. Use the longest panels possible to minimize the number of end joints.
3. Install gypsum wallboard so that the edges and ends are secured to framing except when they are at right angles to the framing members. If the framing members are spaced wider than allowed by code for the panel being used, install blocking at each joint.
4. Hold the wallboard tight against the framing while driving nails or screws.

5. Cut the gypsum wallboard so it fits easily into the space without binding against the other panels.

6. Match similar edges. Abut a tapered long edge to another tapered long edge. Butt a square-cut end to another square-cut end.

7. Whenever possible span from one side of the room to the other with a single-length panel.

8. If there are butt joints, try to have them occur near the walls. They are more noticeable if they occur in the center of the room.

9. Stagger end joints.

10. Drywall board joints should not occur at the sides of openings, such as a door opening. Plan the joint to occur near the center of the opening.

11. Begin fastening the panel in its center and work toward the edges.

12. Set the heads of fasteners just below the surface of the panel but do not tear the paper or crush the core.

13. Remove and replace all incorrectly installed fasteners.

14. Be certain mechanical and electrical outlets, such as electrical boxes, are installed so they project out from the framing a distance equal to the thickness of the drywall.

15. Check to see that framing has been installed to support heavy items, such as lighting fixtures. The drywall should never be used to support loads.

16. Have a helper to lift, hold, and nail the panels.

17. If the framing is not dried to the expected 15 percent moisture content or was thoroughly wetted by heavy runs during construction, it should be allowed to dry before installing drywall. If this is not done, the drywall will develop cracks, seams may develop ridges, and you will get popped fasteners.

18. Drywall is delivered to the site on large trucks that usually have a boom or forklift to unload the pallets. Plan to get the truck as close to the house as possible so the installers do not have to carry the panels across the site. This may require some grading of the site in advance.

19. Delivery of wallboard that must go on a second or third floor is another big problem. It can be lifted with a boom, but provision must be made for an opening in the wall. Seldom are window openings large enough. If they are, then this may work; however, you must ask the carpenters to leave out these windows until the drywall is in place. Another technique is to leave off a piece of sheathing, which is installed after the drywall is in place.

20. Check the studs for bowing and correct this before attempting installation.

21. Check double-framed studs for misalignment. This is a special problem when the door frames are installed and the stud framing is out of line, so the drywall has to bulge out past the jam.

22. In a three-stud corner, consider moving over one of the corner studs (6–1). With conventional framing, there is not enough surface to drive the screws straight into a stud. Consider installing a fourth stud if necessary.

23. Bowing insulation panels that protrude below the face of the ceiling joist or wall studs make it difficult to get the drywall tight to the framing (6–2). While it can be forced between the framing, it will eventually lead to popped fasteners and bowed panels. The solution to this problem is to fur the wall or ceiling with 1 × 3-inch wood strips or metal resilient

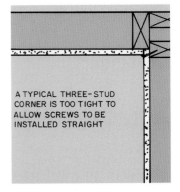

A TYPICAL THREE-STUD CORNER IS TOO TIGHT TO ALLOW SCREWS TO BE INSTALLED STRAIGHT

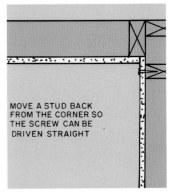

MOVE A STUD BACK FROM THE CORNER SO THE SCREW CAN BE DRIVEN STRAIGHT

▲ 6–1. If you plan to secure both panels to the framing in a typical three-stud inside corner, set them over one of the studs. Consider moving one stud over to provide room to drive the screw straight into the stud.

▲ **6–2.** This exterior wall has been covered with insulation blankets faced with a heavy paper vapor barrier that may bow out beyond the framing.

▲ **6–3.** This wall and ceiling have been insulated with unfaced fiberglass insulation blankets.

▲ **6–4.** This wall was insulated with unfaced insulation blankets and then covered with a plastic sheet vapor barrier.

channel. Secure the drywall to these strips. It is best to insulate with unfaced blankets, which can be easily laid flush with the face of the framing (6–3). Then, staple sheets of plastic vapor barrier over the wall (6–4). Check the insulation around plumbing and electrical outlets and adjust it so it does not interfere with the installation of the drywall (6–5 and 6–6).

24. Consider using adhesive to bond the drywall to the framing and then nail or screw it in place. This increases the cost, but makes a much stronger

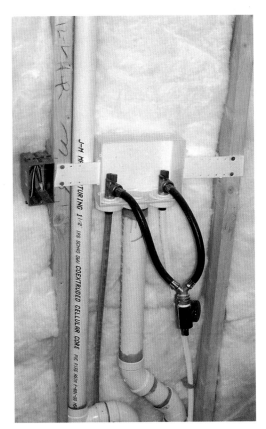

▲ **6–5.** This plumbing installation has insulation placed behind it against the exterior sheathing.

installation and reduces call backs for cracks and nail pops. It also reduces the number of fasteners needed because they can be set on a wider spacing.

25. See Chapter 9 for additional suggestions.

Nailing Patterns

Recommended nailing patterns for gypsum wallboard are detailed in Chapter 5. These include patterns for single nailing with and without the use of adhesives for nails, screws, and staples. Specifications controlling the selection of fasteners are in Chapter 3.

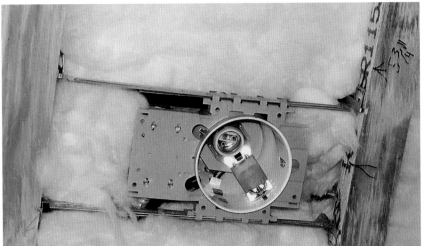

▲ **6–6.** Ceilings often contain electrical outlets for lights, heating and ventilating registers, and other penetrating features that must all be insulated.

Framing Spacing

Recommendations for the maximum allowable framing for single-layer installation are shown in **Table 6–1**. The spacing of the framing and the orientation of the panel to the framing members influences the thickness of wallboard used. Before starting installation, check the framing spacing and the thickness of the wallboard you are expected to install.

TABLE 6–1.
Maximum Recommended Spacing of Framing for Single-Layer Mechanically Applied Gypsum Wallboard

Panel (inches)	Orientation of Panel to Framing	Maximum Framing pacing (inches)
WALLS		
³⁄₈	Parallel or perpendicular	16
¹⁄₂	Parallel or perpendicular	24
⁵⁄₈	Parallel or perpendicular	24
CEILINGS		
³⁄₈	Parallel or perpendicular	16
¹⁄₂	Parallel	16
¹⁄₂	Perpendicular	24
⁵⁄₈	Parallel	16
⁵⁄₈	Perpendicular	24

The carpenters who are framing the building should provide the surfaces needed to back up the drywall for nailing. At the ceiling, blocking or a wide top plate can be used to nail the edges of the ceiling panel (6–7).

When interior partitions meet or butt the exterior wall, there are several framing methods that can be used to provide a nailing surface (6–8).

▶ **6–7.** Some of the ways nailers are installed on top of the partitions.

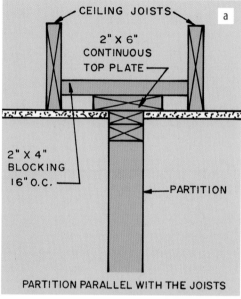

PARTITION PARALLEL WITH THE JOISTS

1. RAISE ONE END UP. THEN LIFT THE OTHER AS YOU STEP ON THE BENCH.

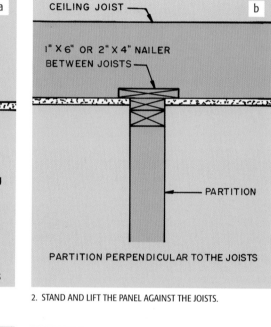

PARTITION PERPENDICULAR TO THE JOISTS

2. STAND AND LIFT THE PANEL AGAINST THE JOISTS.

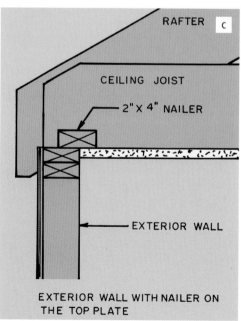

EXTERIOR WALL WITH NAILER ON THE TOP PLATE

3. HOLD THE PANEL FIRMLY AGAINST THE JOISTS AND BEGIN SECURING IT IN PLACE.

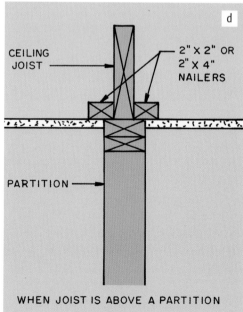

WHEN JOIST IS ABOVE A PARTITION

4. HOLD THE PANEL FIRMLY AGAINST THE JOISTS AND BEGIN SECURING IT IN PLACE.

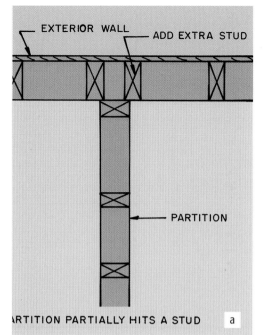

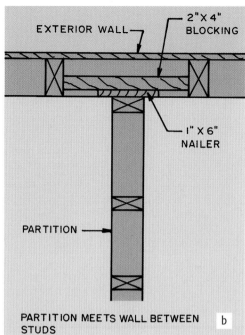

EXTERIOR WALL — ADD EXTRA STUD

PARTITION

PARTITION PARTIALLY HITS A STUD   a

EXTERIOR WALL — 2"X 4" BLOCKING

1" X 6" NAILER

PARTITION —

PARTITION MEETS WALL BETWEEN STUDS   b

▲ **6–8.** Two ways to provide nailers at the points where two partitions meet.

Installing the Ceiling

The gypsum wallboard is installed on the ceiling first. Then the walls are covered. The panels are installed on the ceiling with their **long edge perpendicular** to the joists. The ends should rest on the center of a joist. The panels should be cut to fit to each other with very little space between them. A space of 1/16 inch is considered satisfactory. Use the longest panels possible and keep end joints away from the center of the room when possible.

When the ceiling panels are lifted into place, the location of the joists at the wall is lost. Therefore, mark the center of each joist on the top plate as shown in **6–9**.

It takes two people to lift, hold, and nail ceiling panels. Locate the trestles under the section to be covered. Lift the panel and place one end against the wall or the previous panel. Push it until it is in position and secure the end. The other worker can then lift the panel end up against the framing. Some hold it in place with their heads as they nail it (**6–10**).

The use of a carpenter-made T-brace is another way to hold the panel against the framing. It is made the correct length for the ceiling height (**6–11**). Also, commercially available adjustable T-jacks are available (**6–12**).

An excellent device for lifting and holding ceiling and wall panels is a mechanical panel lift (**6–13**). It is on wheels, so as the panel is lifted it is moved into position and held for nailing by workers on trestles or stilts. It is especially helpful when paneling high cathedral ceilings (**6–14**).

Remember to stagger the butted end joints and try to keep them as near the walls as possible. They are less noticeable if they are around the perimeter of the room.

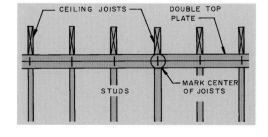

CEILING JOISTS — DOUBLE TOP PLATE

MARK CENTER OF JOISTS

STUDS

◄ **6–9.** Mark the center of each ceiling joist on the top plate so its location is known after the ceiling panel is placed against the joists.

1. RAISE ONE END UP. THEN LIFT THE OTHER AS YOU STEP ON THE BENCH.

2. STAND AND LIFT THE PANEL AGAINST THE JOISTS.

3. HOLD THE PANEL FIRMLY AGAINST THE JOISTS AND BEGIN SECURING IT IN PLACE.

▲ **6–10.** It takes two people to raise and hold a ceiling panel for nailing or screwing to the joists.

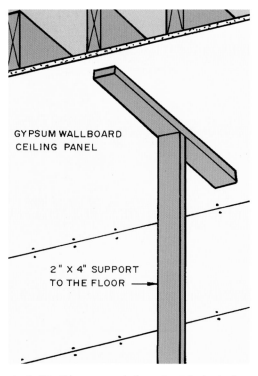

▲ **6-11.** T-braces made from 2 x 4-inch stock can help support the ceiling panel against the joists.

▲ **6-12.** Commercially available panel supports are strong and can be adjusted to various ceiling heights. *(Courtesy Patterson Avenue Tool Co., Inc.)*

▲ **6-13.** This mechanical lift makes it easy to raise and hold panels for nailing or screwing. *(Courtesy Panelift Drywall Lift; photo courtesy Telepro, Inc.)*

◄ **6-14.** The mechanical drywall lift holds panels against the ceiling joists. *(Courtesy Panelift Drywall Lift; photo courtesy Telepro, Inc.)*

Before installing the panels on the ceiling, run a chalkline perpendicular to the joist in several places across the room. Look for joists that are not in the plane of the line. Panels attached to these will produce a wavy finished ceiling. If this cannot be corrected by planing a little off the joists, install 1 × 3-inch wood furring strips across them. The strips can be set into the same plane by driving wedges behind the strips. The panels are nailed to the furring in the same manner as joists.

When hanging a cathedral ceiling without using a mechanical panel lift, install the first panel next to the wall. This will allow the second row to slide down against it and be supported by the edge of the first panel. When using a mechanical lift, some people prefer to install the top panel first, as shown in **6–14**.

LOCATING THE PANELS

Begin by installing one panel in the corner of the room (**6–15**). Be certain it does not extend past the center of the joist on which the end rests. Trim as necessary to fit in place. Then install the second panel. Depending on the room size, it may have to be cut to length. The edge of the board does not have to fit

tight to the top plate. A space of ⅛ to ¼ inch will be covered by the wall panel and allow room for possible expansion. Continue across the room.

Now measure and cut the first piece for the second row. Be certain you keep the end joint several feet away from the first joint. Continue this process keeping the end joints staggered. If it is possible, use full-length panels (such as a 12-foot panel in rooms up to 12 feet wide). This will give a ceiling with no end joints.

Remember to locate and cut out any openings required, such as for an electrical box for a light or ceiling fan.

NAILING THE CEILING PANELS

Begin nailing in the center of the panel and work toward the edges. This enables the installer to get the panel flat against the joists and prevents possible bowing, which can occur if the perimeter is nailed first. The ceiling panel may be either single- or double-nailed. Whenever possible, it is always best to double-nail. Detailed patterns for fastening with nails and screws are explained in Chapter 5.

Gypsum wallboard manufacturers recommend that the edges of ceiling panels next to the wall not be nailed. This allows for movement between

▶ **6–15.** Install the first panel in a corner and finish that row across the room. Plan to use a 12-foot panel in the center of the next row to get the end joints near the wall. When all panels are installed, go back over them and check for loose spots, torn paper, and other defects that should be repaired.

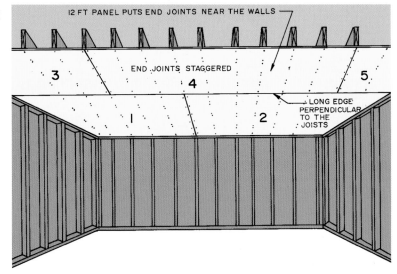

12 FT PANEL PUTS END JOINTS NEAR THE WALLS

END JOINTS STAGGERED

3   4   5

LONG EDGE PERPENDICULAR TO THE JOISTS

1   2

the wall and joists. Since the wall panels butt up against the ceiling panel, it is supported by them. This is called a floating angle (**6–16**).

Ceiling panels running perpendicular to the joists may be installed with adhesive and nails. Apply a ⅜-inch-wide bead of adhesive to the joists as shown in Chapter 5. Space the nails 16 inches O.C. on each end of the panel and 24 inches O.C. along the ceiling joists on the panel field.

Installing Single-Layer Wall Panels

After the framing has been checked and corrected for straightness, the wall panel installation can begin. Remember to check the insulation. It should be stapled to the inside of the studs, not to the faces.

The first decision you must make is whether to install the panels horizontally or vertically. If the ceiling is 8 feet high, horizontal installation will produce fewer joints. However, they can be installed vertically if you wish. The horizontal method is best if single panels can cover the wall from one side of the room to the other. This produces only an edge joint and no end joints.

If ceiling heights are over 8 feet, apply the panels vertically or use a special 54-inch-wide panel (**6–17**). This eliminates a wide fill-in strip and a lot of extra, difficult taping and finishing. This is especially useful for 9-foot ceilings. Most prefer to put the narrow strip down by the floor.

Begin by installing the top row of panels (**6–18**). After the top row is completed around the entire room, you

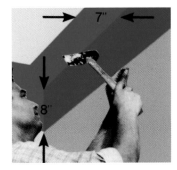

▲ **6–16.** No nails are to be in the ceiling closer than 7 inches from the wall, and in the wall panel 8 inches from the ceiling. This creates what is referred to as a floating angle. (*Courtesy National Gypsum Company.*)

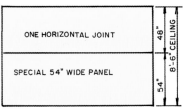

ONE HORIZONTAL JOINT — 48"

SPECIAL 54" WIDE PANEL — 54"

8'-6" CEILING

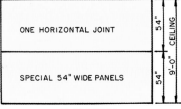

ONE HORIZONTAL JOINT — 54"

SPECIAL 54" WIDE PANELS — 54"

9'-0" CEILING

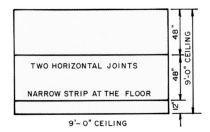

TWO HORIZONTAL JOINTS — 48" 48"

NARROW STRIP AT THE FLOOR — 12"

9'-0" CEILING

▲ **6–17.** Typical plans for wall installation in rooms with 8'6" and 9'0" ceilings. Use a wider panel whenever it will eliminate one edge joint. When using the 48-inch width, many installers prefer to place the narrow strip next to the floor.

1. RAISE THE PANEL UP ON THE WALL.

2. SECURE THE PANEL IN PLACE AND THEN INSTALL THE NEXT TOP PANEL.

◄ **6–18.** Install the top row of wall panels first.

▶ **6–19.** After installing a panel that lays over an opening, such as a door or window, carefully mark and cut away the overlapping piece.

▲ **6–20.** A drywall lifter will help raise the bottom panel an inch or so, leaving both hands free to fasten the panel to the framing.

can place the lower row. Be certain to stagger the end joints. When a panel overlays an opening, carefully mark and cut away the overlaying piece. End joints should fall over the opening, not at a corner (**6–19**). The lower panels can be lifted an inch or so with a drywall lifter. Place the panel on the top of the lifter, slide your foot back, and carefully press down on your heel to raise the panel (**6–20**).

You must never allow an end joint to occur at the corner of a wall opening. The stresses here will cause the wall to eventually crack. Plan the panels so the joint occurs near the center of the opening as shown in **6–21**. The carpenter should have placed studs and cripples

every 16 or 24 inches so that the nailing surface is there. Do not nail the panel to the header over the opening.

Remember to locate and cut the openings for light switches and outlets, as well as plumbing and mechanical system requirements.

SECURING THE PANELS

Panels can be secured to wood framing with nails or screws, and to metal framing with screws. Screws are the best because they are rapidly installed, more secure, and fewer fasteners are required. Recommended fastener spacing is shown in **Tables 6–2** and **6–3**. Additional information on fasteners is in Chapter 5.

TABLE 6–2
Fastener Spacing Without Adhesive*

Framing	Framing Spacing (inches)	Maximum Fastener Spacing (inches)		Framing Spacing (inches)	Maximum Fastener Spacing (inches)	
Wall	16" OC	Nails	Screws	24" OC	Nails	Screws
		8	16		8	12
Ceiling	16" OC	7	12	24" OC	7	12

*Mechanically attached, single layer

GYPSUM WALLBOARD INSTALLATION

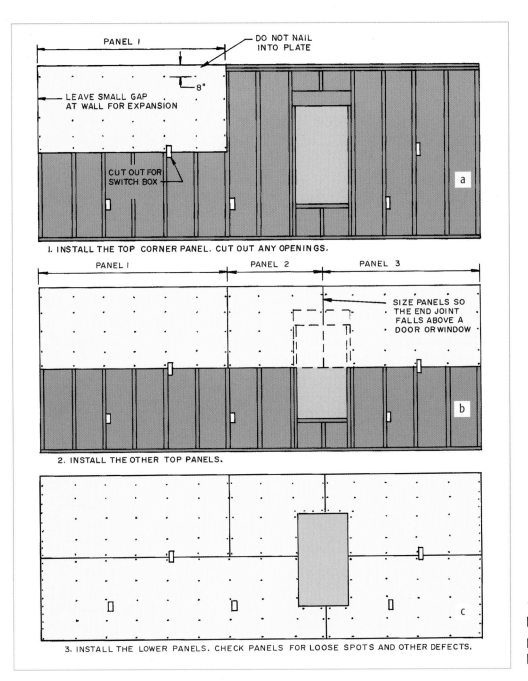

PANEL 1

DO NOT NAIL INTO PLATE

8"

LEAVE SMALL GAP AT WALL FOR EXPANSION

CUT OUT FOR SWITCH BOX

a

1. INSTALL THE TOP CORNER PANEL. CUT OUT ANY OPENINGS.

PANEL 1   PANEL 2   PANEL 3

SIZE PANELS SO THE END JOINT FALLS ABOVE A DOOR OR WINDOW

b

2. INSTALL THE OTHER TOP PANELS.

c

3. INSTALL THE LOWER PANELS. CHECK PANELS FOR LOOSE SPOTS AND OTHER DEFECTS.

◀ **6–21.** When hanging a wall, begin by installing a top row of panels. Complete each row before you hang the row below it.

TABLE 6–3
Fastener Spacing with Adhesive*

Framing	Framing Spacing (inches)	Maximum Fastener Spacing (inches)		Framing Spacing (inches)	Maximum Fastener Spacing (inches)	
Wall	16" OC	Nails	Screws	24	Nails	Screws
		16	24		16	24
Ceiling	16" OC	16	16	24	12	16

*Single-layer panel

▶ **6–22.** Typical floating interior corners at the ceiling. Omit the fasteners in the top edge of each panel.

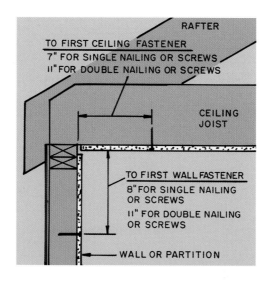

▶ **6–23.** Typical floating interior wall panels in a corner. Omit the fasteners in the panel that is butted by the meeting panel.

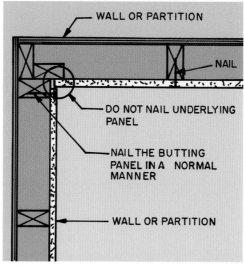

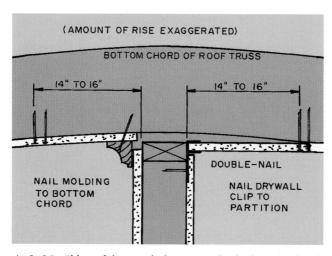

▲ **6–24.** Either of these techniques permits the bottom chord of the truss to rise without causing a major crack in the drywall at the ceiling.

Floating Interior-Angle Construction

Floating interior-angle construction is a method used to reduce cracking and nail pops caused by stresses that develop at wall-to-wall and wall-to-ceiling intersections. You do not install fasteners on one of the panels at each interior angle. The panels need wood backup blocking just the same as if they were to be nailed. When a wall panel meets a ceiling panel, the last fastener in the ceiling panel should be 7 inches from the wall for single nailing and 11 inches for double nailing (**6–22**). When nailing the wall panels near the ceiling, the top fastener should be 8 inches from the ceiling for single nailing and 11 inches for double nailing.

The nailing of wall panels forming an interior corner is shown in **6–23**. The fasteners are omitted in the panel that is behind the butting panel. The butting panel is nailed in the usual manner.

Coping with Truss Rise

The bottom chord of roof trusses can arch upward if the moisture content in the top and bottom chords is different. This causes cracks between the ceiling and the wall. The typical taped ceiling-wall corner is not strong enough to resist the stress and will not move, so it cracks. A variation of the floating corner to handle possible truss rise is shown in **6–24**.

Control Joints

Control joints are used to prevent cracking in large areas of gypsum wallboard. For example, when the wall exceeds one floor in height it is recommended that a horizontal control joint be installed between the gypsum panels along the line created when the first-floor studs butt the double top plate (**6–25**).

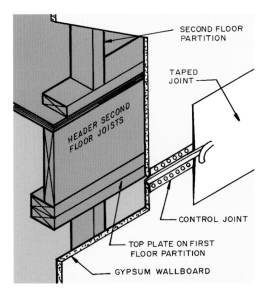

▲ **6–25.** When installing high walls, place an extension joint below the second-floor joist header.

The gypsum panels should not be nailed to the side face of joists or headers. The control joint permits some movement of the gypsum panels (**6–26**). Typically, control joints are used on long partitions, such as a long hall, when it is at least 30 feet. On ceilings, they are used every 50 feet and the total area should not exceed 3,500 square feet.

The control joint is installed after the panels are in place. A space is left between them into which the joint fits. It is nailed or stapled every 6 inches along each flange. Tape is laid over the flanges in the normal manner, and joint compound is applied in finish coats, as is done on other taping jobs. The control joint has paper tear-off strips that are removed after the taping is finished, leaving an open channel. If fire or sound control are factors, a seal must be placed behind the control joint.

It is recommended that control joints be used in ceilings over 2,500 square feet and in walls over 30 feet in length. They are secured to the gypsum wallboard with 9/16-inch staples or nailed every 6 inches along each flange.

Installing Drywall on Gable Walls

Cathedral ceilings are popular—which means you will have to hang drywall on gable walls. This calls for careful measuring of the length of the panel so it ends on a stud for laying out the angle on the end to match the roof slope. It may be economical to install extra studs for the end of panels on the gable end so the full length of the panel can be used. This will often eliminate one end joint.

Start by installing the panels from the floor. The first panel that touches the ceiling should have part of its end vertical and the rest should be sloped (**6–27**, panel 3) to fit the ceiling. While designs may vary, it is typical to start an 8'-0" wall with a 24-inch-wide panel (panel 1), followed by a 48-inch panel (**6–27**, panel 2). This makes the third row meet the requirements just mentioned. It goes without saying that you will have installed the ceiling panels before doing the gable end. Remember to install control joints if conditions require it. (See **6–25** and **6–26**.)

To lay out the first sloped panel (panel 3), place the T-square on the top of the wall panel as shown in **6–28**. Slide it until the end touches the drywall ceiling. Measure distances A and B.

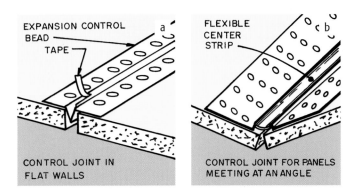

▲ **6–26.** Two types of control joints when the area covered is large. They limit the possibility of damage due to expansion and contraction.

▶ **6–27.** This is a suggested way to plan a panel layout for hanging a gable end that has a cathedral ceiling. Remember to consider using expansion joints if the area is large.

FIRST GABLE END PANEL TO CONTACT SLOPED CEILING

PANEL 4

PANEL 3

PANEL 2

PANEL I

INSTALL THIS PANEL FIRST

4'-0"

4'-0"

2'-0"

8'-0"

▼ **6–28.** These are the steps to follow to locate the cut at the panel end that butts the sloped ceiling.

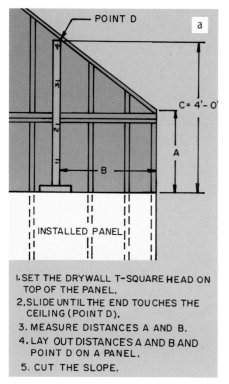

POINT D

C = 4'-0"

A

B

INSTALLED PANEL

1. SET THE DRYWALL T-SQUARE HEAD ON TOP OF THE PANEL.
2. SLIDE UNTIL THE END TOUCHES THE CEILING (POINT D).
3. MEASURE DISTANCES A AND B.
4. LAY OUT DISTANCES A AND B AND POINT D ON A PANEL.
5. CUT THE SLOPE.

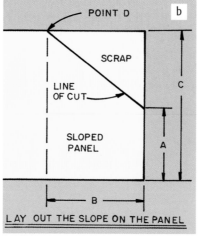

POINT D

b

SCRAP

LINE OF CUT

SLOPED PANEL

C

A

B

LAY OUT THE SLOPE ON THE PANEL

Measure these on the panel and cut the angle (6–28). Then measure the length and mark and cut if necessary so the end rests on a stud. The other pieces can be laid out in the same manner, except the entire end will slope.

Installing Drywall on Stair Walls

A stair wall will contain the first-floor studs, header, joists for the second floor, and the second-floor studs. Begin the first panel at the ceiling. While the sizes will vary—some depending on the height of the wall—you want to avoid having an edge joint occur at the top plate of the first floor wall. It is likely there will be more movement here, and it's best if you cover it over with a solid panel. Refer to 6–29 and you will see a typical situation. If using 54-inch-wide panels helps reduce the number of edge joints, by all means do so. As the drywall gets low enough to hit the stair, the end may be cut on the angle of the stair, but generally, it is run to the floor behind the stair stringer. The stair stringer rests against the drywall and the finish stringer is nailed over the drywall (6–30). If the stair stringers are installed before the drywall, the carpenter will usually set the wall stringer out ½ inch to allow the drywall to fit behind it.

Refer back to the recommendations for using a control joint. The line of the top of the first-floor top plate is a typical location on a high wall.

Installing Drywall on Furred-Down Areas

The ceiling is often furred down above kitchen cabinets, as well as built-in cabinets in the living room, bathroom, and other areas of the house. The carpenter will have constructed the framing, which goes above the cabinets. Your job is to hang the wall up to the furred-down area and then cover this area. If it is a kitchen, most of the wall will be covered with the base cabinet and the wall cabinet. Usually the wall cabinets will have a back, so the drywall behind them is not seen. The base cabinets usually are open on the back. Remember, also, that there are a string of electrical outlets located just above the counter top and often a telephone outlet as well. A typical situation is shown in 6–31.

A good way to begin is to install a panel on the wall below the furred-down area (6–32). This will produce one edge joint beneath the base cabinet. Remember to cut holes for the plumbing and electrical outlets. Complete covering the wall before you cover the furred-down area.

Next, cover the bottom of the furred-down area. Usually it is wider than the

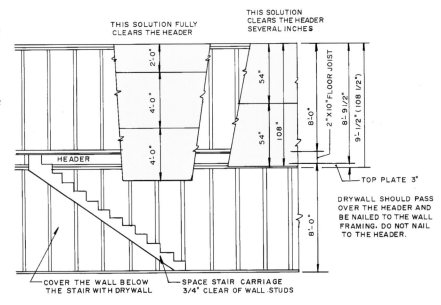

▲ **6–29.** Two possible ways to hang a wall on a stair. The panel should pass over the header of the second floor and not be nailed to it.

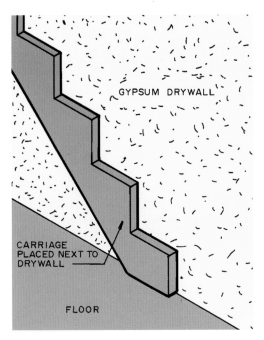

▲ **6–30.** Typically, drywall is run behind the stair carriage and down to the floor.

▶ **6–31.** Typical sizes for kitchen cabinets. These produce a 12-inch furred-down area at the ceiling.

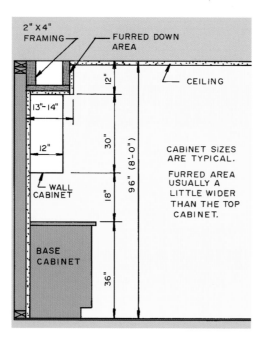

wall cabinets, so a clean, sharp corner is needed. And finally, cover the remainder, check for loose nails or torn paper, and you are ready to finish as shown in **6–33**.

Installing Panels on Out-of-Plumb Walls

When a wall is out of plumb, the square end of the butting panel will not meet it properly. To handle this place the panel against the wall, and place a board, such as a 1 × 4, against the out-of-plumb wall. Mark along the edge, locating a line that is parallel with the wall. After cutting this sloped end, measure and cut the length of the panel (**6–34**).

Double-Layer Wallboard Installation

Double-layer installation provides additional fire protection and reduces the amount of sound that can pass through the partition. The first layer is nailed or screwed to the framing using the same spacing as single-layer. The base may have the long joints vertical or horizontal. The face layer must have the long joints perpendicular to those on the base layer (**6–35**). The face layer is bonded to the base with adhesive and fastened with enough fasteners as needed to hold it tight as the adhesive sets. (See Chapter 5 for information on nails, screws, and adhesive.)

Installing Drywall on Curved Walls and Arches

It takes careful work and planning to hang curved walls and arches. First of all the carpenter should have properly prepared the framing. The space between wall studs and other framing material is

▶ **6–32.** Hang the wall below the furred-down area before you cover it with drywall. This design puts the horizontal joint behind the base cabinets.

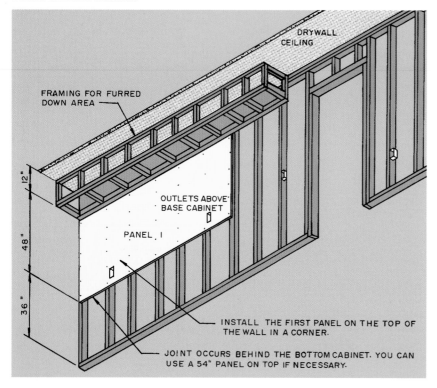

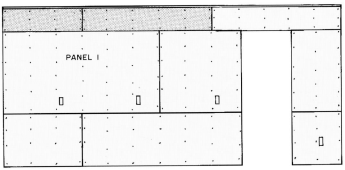

2. THEN COVER THE FURRED DOWN AREA.

PANEL 1

1. FINISH HANGING THE WALL.

◀ **6-33.** After the wall has been covered, hang the drywall on the furred-down area.

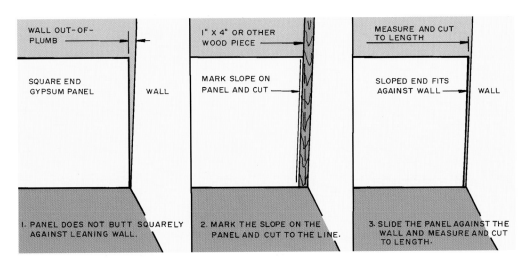

WALL OUT-OF-PLUMB

SQUARE END GYPSUM PANEL

WALL

1. PANEL DOES NOT BUTT SQUARELY AGAINST LEANING WALL.

1" X 4" OR OTHER WOOD PIECE

MARK SLOPE ON PANEL AND CUT

2. MARK THE SLOPE ON THE PANEL AND CUT TO THE LINE.

MEASURE AND CUT TO LENGTH

SLOPED END FITS AGAINST WALL

WALL

3. SLIDE THE PANEL AGAINST THE WALL AND MEASURE AND CUT TO LENGTH.

◀ **6-34.** These are the steps to follow when a panel butts a wall that is out of plumb.

▼ **6-35.** Double-layer construction requires that the long edge of the panels in each layer be perpendicular to each other.

very important. If the space is too great, the wall will have a series of flat surfaces.

Hanging Panels on Curved Walls

It is recommended that you use a special ¼-inch flexible gypsum panel designed for curved surface installation. This is a two-layer installation with a second ¼-inch panel overlaid on the first. Typical bending radii for ¼-inch High-Flex wallboard, manufactured by National Gypsum Company, are given in **Table 6–4**. Consult the manufacturer of the product you will be using for specific technical data.

This product is significantly more flexible if installed with the long edges in the vertical position. For instance, notice

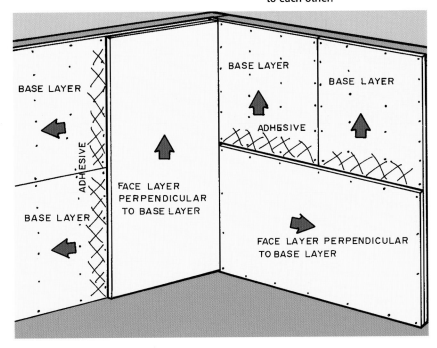

BASE LAYER

ADHESIVE

BASE LAYER

FACE LAYER PERPENDICULAR TO BASE LAYER

BASE LAYER

BASE LAYER

ADHESIVE

FACE LAYER PERPENDICULAR TO BASE LAYER

▲ **6–37.** The track is formed to the radius of the curved wall and secured to the floor. The studs are screwed to the track. *(Courtesy Radius Track Corp.)*

▲ **6–38.** The curved track is installed on top of the wall studs serving as a top plate. *(Courtesy Radius Track Corp.)*

▲ **6–36.** This flexible track is used to align studs that form curved walls and to frame arched openings. *(Courtesy Radius Track Corp.)*

in **Table 6–4** that when applied widthwise (width perpendicular to the studs) the minimum bend radii are considerably smaller. Critical to a good job is the spacing of the studs, also shown in **Table 6–4**. When fastening the panels, they must be held in firm contact with the framing member as the fasteners are being driven.

There are various commercial products available for use to form the base and top of curved walls and for forming arches. One such product is shown in **6–36**. To form a curved wall, the track is easily formed to the radius of the curve and secured to the floor (**6–37**). As the studs are screwed to the track, a second section is placed like a top plate and the studs are screwed to it (**6–38**). This allows the wall to go up fast, reducing labor costs.

When covering **concave surfaces**, place a wood stop at one end of the curve and press the panel against it from the other edge. This helps bow the panel to the wall. Start installing the fasteners from the end against the stop (**6–39**).

Some prefer to start nailing a panel on a concave wall by starting in the center and working toward each end.

When installing on **convex surfaces**, first nail one end to the framing with nails or screws. Then push the panel against the framing nailing toward the loose end (**6–40**).

TABLE 6–4.
Minimum Bending Radii for ¼-inch High-Flex Wallboard

	LENGTHWISE		WIDTHWISE	
Application	**Bend Radii**	**Max. Stud Spacing**	**Bend Radii**	**Max. Stud Spacing**
Inside (concave)	32"	9" O.C.	20"	9" O.C.
Outside (convex)	30"	9" O.C.	15"	8" O.C.
Inside (concave)	20"	9" O.C.	10"	6" O.C.
Outside (convex)	14"	6" O.C.	7"	5" O.C.

(Courtesy National Gypsum Company)

GYPSUM WALLBOARD INSTALLATION

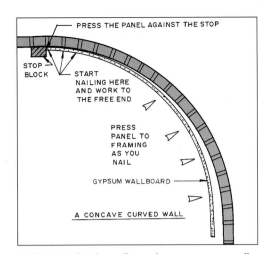

▲ **6–39.** The drywall panel on a concave wall can be installed by nailing on one end and working toward the free end, keeping the panel tight to the framing. Some people prefer to start in the center and nail toward each end.

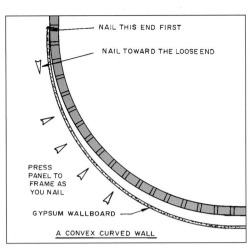

▲ **6–40.** The drywall panel on a convex curved wall can be installed by starting to nail at one end and pressing firmly against the frame as you nail to the free end.

If curves with smaller radii are to be covered, or if ½-inch drywall is to be used, apply 20 to 30 ounces of water to the back of the panel with a roller or fine spray. Permit it to soak 30 to 60 minutes before installing. Too much water can damage the panel and may cause blistering. When the temperature is at 65°F (18°C) or the air has a humidity of 45 percent or less, the addition of moisture to the panel will be helpful.

When regular gypsum wallboard is used on curved walls, it's possible to achieve much larger radii than with flexible panels. Examples of bend radii are given in **Table 6–4**.

When standard gypsum panels are to be used, you can introduce a natural bend by placing the ends on two objects with a weight in the center, and letting them sit like this for a day or two. This natural bend will help when placing them on the wall (**6–41**).

Another technique is to dampen the back of the panel by rolling on the water with a paint roller. However, this is a bit difficult because too much water will cause the paper to loosen, and then, when dry, to form blisters. Let the wet panels set for about an hour before installing them, and allow them to dry at least 24 hours before taping.

Either wood or metal studs can be used for curved walls. When wood is used, the studs are nailed to the floor and curved wood blocking is nailed between them, serving as a bottom plate (**6–42**). When metal studs are used, the bottom runner is made to bend to the desired radius and the metal studs are set in the runner.

Install the panels in the same manner as other walls. Using screws can be a big help in stabilizing the installation. Be careful in nailing or screwing, because the panel will not necessarily always be flat against the stud. Nail into the edge of the stud touching the panel.

Place the fasteners no farther than 12 inches O.C. Be certain to stagger the

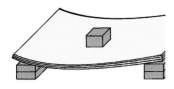

▲ **6–41.** Some permanent bow can be placed in panels by holding up the ends, placing a weight in the center, and letting them sit for 18 to 24 hours.

TABLE 6–5
Minimum Bending Radii of Dry Standard Gypsum Wallboard

MINIMUM BENDING RADII OF DRY GYPSUM BOARD					
Board Thickness		**Board Applied with Long Dimension Perpendicular to Framing**		**Board Applied with Long Dimension Parallel to Framing**	
in.	mm	ft.	m	ft.	m
½	12.7	20 (1)	6.1	–	–
⅜	9.5	7.5	2.3	25	7.6
¼	6.4	5	1.5	15	4.6

(1) Bending two ¼-inch pieces successively permits radii shown for ½-inch gypsum board.

Minimum Bending Radii of Wetted Standard Gypsum Wallboard [1]

Board Thickness	**Min. Radius**	**Length of Arc**	**No. of Studs on Arc and Tangents** [3]	**Approx. Stud Spacing**	**Max. Stud Spacing**	**Water Required per Panel**
(inches)	(feet)	(feet) [2]	inches [4]	(inches) [4]	Side (ounces) [5]	m
¼	2	3.14	9	5.50	6	30
¼	2.5	3.93	10	5.93	6	30
⅜	3	4.71	9	7.85	8	35
⅜	3.5	5.50	11	7.22	8	35
½	4	6.28	8	11.70	12	45
½	4.5	7.07	9	11.40	12	45

(1) For gypsum board applied horizontally to a 4-inch partition.
(2) Arc length = 3.24R/2 (for a 90-degree arc).
(3) No. studs = outside arc length/maximum spacing +1 (rounded up to the next whole number).
(4) Stud spacing + outside arc length/no, of studs -1 (measured along outside of runner).
(5) Wet only the side of board that will be in tension. Water required per board side is based on 4' x 8' sheet.
(Courtesy United States Gypsum Corporation)

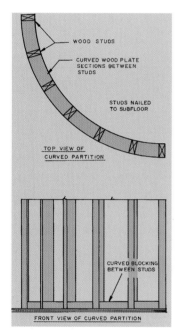

▲ **6–42.** A curved wall with wood studs can be framed by keeping them close together, as shown in **6–39** and **6–40**. Cut curved wood blocking and nail between the studs at the floor.

joints on the second layer away from those on the first layer. If possible, use panels that are long enough to make the curve without end joints. It is best to avoid end joints; end joints in a curve are very hard to finish.

Joints on curved walls are finished with paper tape and three coats of joint compound.

Installing Arches

Arches are widely used for interior partition openings, and add grace and beauty to the partition and the room (**6–43**).

Arches can be carpenter-built using plywood panels and 2 × 4-inch blocking,

as shown in **6–44**. It is important that the frame that's built has an adequate nailing surface. The arch is then covered with High-Flex gypsum wallboard. Bending radii are shown in **Table 6–4**. If regular gypsum wallboard is used, it will not bend around the arch unless it is scored every ½, ¾, or 1 inch on the back. The smaller the arch, the closer together the score marks. As the panel is nailed in place, the score marks open, allowing the panel to fit around the arched opening (**6–45**).

The use of ¼-inch High-Flex gypsum board permits most arches to be covered by simply bending the panel around the arch. Start fastening in the center and work toward each end. It can be lightly wetted as explained earlier, if the arch is

▲ **6–43.** Arches form a dramatic interior design feature.

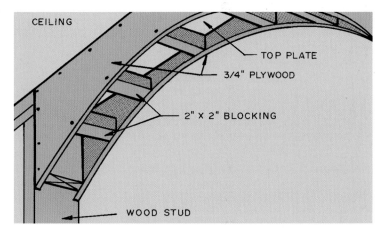

▲ **6–44.** The carpenter will frame the arched opening with plywood panels and wood blocking.

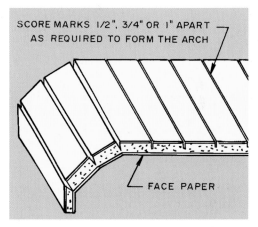

◀ **6–45.** Regular gypsum wallboard will usually have to be scored on the back before it will bend around the arch.

small (**6–46**). Both the regular and High-Flex panels require the edge to be covered with a corner bead.

A faster and easier way to form arches is to use a track built for that purpose. A short arch formed with track is shown in **6–47**. Notice that it overlaps the side studs and is screwed to them. In the center, it is screwed to the framing over the opening. A much larger arch is shown in **6–48**. The drywall is secured to the track with drywall screws that drill right into the track. After the gypsum drywall has been secured to the track and framing, the edges are covered with a corner bead and finished in the normal manner (**6–49**).

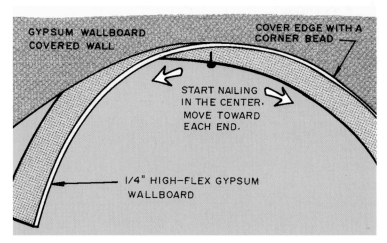

▲ **6–46.** High-Flex gypsum wallboard will bend around arches as small as 30 inches when installed dry, and 20 inches when wetted.

▶ **6–47.** This short arch was formed with a flexible track. The drywall is screwed to the track. *(Courtesy Radius Track Corp.)*

▲ **6–48.** This large deep arch track is screwed to the studs on the sides and has 2 × 4-inch cripples secured across the top. *(Courtesy Radius Track Corp.)*

▲ **6–49.** After the drywall has been installed, the edges of the arches are covered with corner bead and finished with drywall tape and joint compound.

Installing Predecorated Gypsum Panels

Predecorated gypsum panels have some form of finished surface applied during their manufacture. It is typically a vinyl or fabric covering, or a painted or other type of liquid coating applied to provide either a smooth or textured surface.

Before installing the wall panels, finish the ceiling, and tape and sand it so all dust and tool work is complete. Some prefer to paint the ceiling at this point so there is no danger of splattering the walls.

The easiest way to install predecorated panels is to place them in a vertical position and nail to the studs with colored nails supplied by the manufacturer. Use a plastic-headed hammer. The color helps the nails blend into the panel. The panels are typically ½ inch thick and the nails supplied are 1⅜ inches long. Nail them ⅜ inch from the edge and 8 inches O.C. on the edges and in the field of the panel.

Since the panels are available in lengths of up to 10 feet, you can apply them vertically so no end joints occur. Cut the panels to length with a very sharp utility knife in the same manner as regular gypsum panels.

Because there can be some variation in the decorative surface, you should line up a series of panels against the wall and rearrange them to get the appearance you like.

Joints are covered with a variety of moldings supplied by the manufacturer. Some examples are shown in **6–50**. The snap-on panels have base strip that is nailed or screwed every 12 inches O.C. to the framing. The colored trim is pressed against it and snaps over the sides. These vinyl trim pieces are best cut with a fine-toothed hacksaw. The cuts can be smoothed with a fine-toothed file or sandpaper.

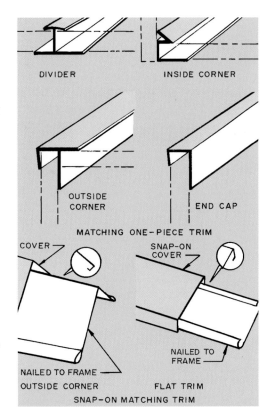

▲ **6–50.** Examples of one-piece trim and snap-on matching trim used with predecorated drywall panels.

Tile Wallcovering

Walls that will be finished with ceramic tile should be covered with moisture-resistant gypsum panels, water-resistant gypsum panels, or cement board. Moisture-resistant panels are used in areas of light moisture exposure, while water-resistant gypsum panels and cement board are used in areas of high humidity or where the tile will be directly exposed to water. See Chapter 3 for detailed information on these products.

INSTALLING MOISTURE-RESISTANT GYPSUM WALLBOARD

Walls in areas where moisture is likely to be present, such as rooms with high humidity or where water will be used, can be covered with moisture-resistant

▲ **6–51.** Moisture-resistant gypsum wallboard is installed on the walls in areas where there will be some humidity and, in some cases, where ceramic tile will be installed.

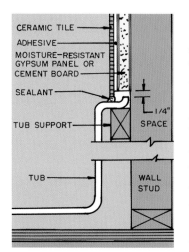

▲ **6–52.** An installation detail for water-resistant gypsum wallboard used as a base for ceramic tile around a bathtub. *(Courtesy National Gypsum Company)*

gypsum panels (6–51). The panels usually extend beyond the area to be tiled, such as around a lavatory, and cover the entire lower wall. They are installed in the manner described for standard gypsum wallboard. The use of screws is recommended, and using tile adhesive eliminates the need for tape, edge sealants filling the edge tapers, or spotting the fasteners. Use the adhesive recommended by the manufacturer. Some people seal the paper face with a water-resistant sealant recommended by the manufacturer.

INSTALLING WATER-RESISTANT GYPSUM PANELS

These gypsum panels are secured to the studs and ceiling joists. Do not install a vapor barrier behind them. If a thin ceramic tile is to be used, the panels can be nailed 8 inches OC. If a thick, heavy tile is used, space the nails 4 inches OC. Screws are spaced 8 inches OC. Some people also apply an adhesive to the framing.

When installing the panels, leave a ¼-inch space between the edges of the panels and the tub or shower, as shown in 6–52 and 6–53. A bead of water-resistant adhesive caulking is laid out in this space, sealing the panel to the fixture. The nails and screws are covered with a water-resistant adhesive.

Fill the joints and any other openings, such as faucets penetrating the panel, with a water-resistant caulk. Then tape the joints with an adhesive-backed fiberglass-mesh joint tape. Apply two coats of water-resistant joint compound over the tape. Since water-resistant gypsum panels have a glass mat bonded to the surface, no surface sealing is necessary.

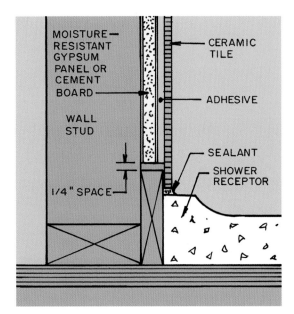

▲ **6–53.** This shows the installation of water-resistant gypsum wallboard as a base for a shower wall with ceramic tile. *(Courtesy National Gypsum Company)*

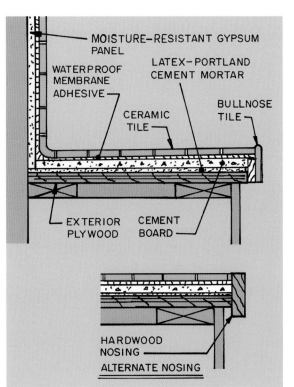

▲ **6–54.** Cement board is used as the wall covering or underlayment on tile-covered countertop because it resists damage from direct contact of water.

INSTALLING CEMENT BOARD

Cement board is installed perpendicular to the studs and ceiling joists. It is attached with special galvanized nails or screws designed for attaching cement board to wood and metal framing. Usually a construction adhesive is applied to the framing, providing additional strength. Place the smooth side facing the room if ceramic tile is to be bonded with an adhesive, or the rough side facing the room if a thin-set mortar is to be used as a tile bonding agent. Space the nails or screws 8 inches O.C. Set them in at least ⅜ inch but not more than ⅝ inch from the edges of the panel. See Chapter 5 for information on cutting cement board to length and cutting openings.

Cement board can also be used as the underlayment on countertops with an approved construction adhesive and secured with screws or nails prepared for use with cement board. They are spaced 8 inches O.C. around the edges of the panel and in the field.

TUB AND SHOWER WALL TILE INSTALLATION

Tubs, tubs with showers, and self-contained showers must have water-resistant gypsum drywall or cement board panels mounted on the studs. The panel edges and fasteners must be coated with a manufactured adhesive. Maintain a ¼-inch space between the lower edge of the panels and the tub or shower as shown in 6–53 and 6–54.

1. SHIMMING ENSURES THAT THE TUB LIP WILL BE IN THE SAME PLANE AS THE INSTALLED MOISTURE-RESISTANT WALLBOARD.

2. A QUARTER-INCH SHIM IS USED TO CREATE NECESSARY SPACE BETWEEN THE WALLBOARD AND TUB.

3. THE MOISTURE-RESISTANT WALLBOARD IS APPLIED TO STUDS IN THE SAME WAY AS GYPSUM WALLBOARD.

4. WATER-RESISTANT TILE ADHESIVE OR ELASTOMERIC CAULKING COMPOUND IS APPLIED AROUND CUT-OUTS AND THE TUB LIP.

▲ **6–55.** Steps for installing water-resistant gypsum around a bathtub. *(Courtesy National Gypsum Company)*

A bead of water-resistant adhesive is laid on the tub or shower lip and on all corners and openings where water pipes penetrate the wall. A series of steps for preparing a bathtub are shown in **6–55.**

Installing Trim and Corner Beads

7

VARIOUS TYPES OF METAL AND *vinyl trim materials are available. They are used to finish and conceal the edges of gypsum wallboard. They protect corners from impact damage, and provide a straight raised edge for taping and finishing corners. Proper selection and installation are critical to producing a professionally finished job. This chapter shows only a few of the many types of corner beads available. Some are for special installation situations, as when a reveal is wanted. Consult the catalogues of trim manufacturers for a complete listing.*

The procedure for finishing beads is discussed in Chapter 10.

Trim

Trim includes accessories used to cover the edges of gypsum wallboard where the edge of an opening or some other feature is exposed. The trim may be metal or plastic. It is placed over the gypsum panel, and nails are driven through its flange, the gypsum panel, and into the stud. Nails are spaced 9 inches O.C. The flange is then finished with several coats of finishing compound. You can see some examples in 7–1.

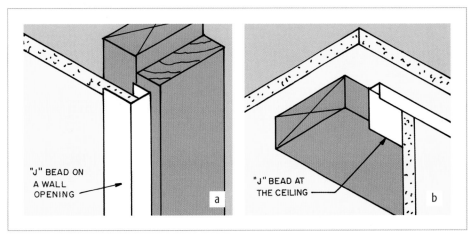

▲ 7–1. Trim is used to cover the raw exposed edges of gypsum wallboard.

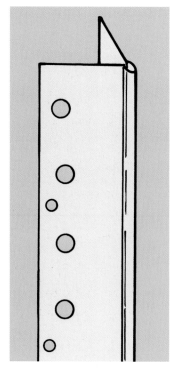

▲ **7–2.** This is a typical type of metal corner bead. It is made of galvanized steel.

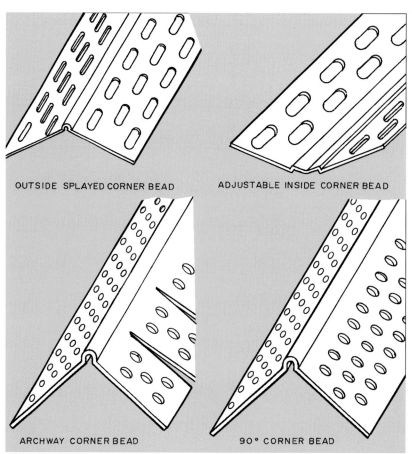

OUTSIDE SPLAYED CORNER BEAD

ADJUSTABLE INSIDE CORNER BEAD

ARCHWAY CORNER BEAD

90° CORNER BEAD

▲ **7–3.** Some of the frequently used vinyl corner beads. *(Courtesy Trim-Tex, Inc.)*

BULLNOSE CORNER BEAD

▲ **7–4.** A vinyl bullnose corner bead is flexible and can be bent around a corner to form a rounded corner surface.

(Courtesy Trim-Tex, Inc.)

Corner Beads

Corner beads are used to reinforce and finish external corners on walls, soffits, pilasters, beams, and columns. Metal and vinyl types are available. A typical metal bead is shown in 7–2, and commonly used vinyl beads are shown in 7–3. The vinyl bullnose bead in 7–4 provides a broadly rounded corner. A paper-faced vinyl bead is shown in 7–5, and a paper-faced metal bead is shown in 7–6. There are a number of special beads used to turn corners. Those shown in 7–7 are for finishing inside and outside corners. There are many other special bead designs available. Consult the catalog of the manufacturer for additional information.

INSTALLATION TECHNIQUES

It is important that the gypsum board forming the corner is straight and smooth. Before installing corner beads, be certain that one of the butting panels does not extend out beyond the face of the other panel, depthwise. If it does, trim it back, and it's okay if it winds up a little more shallow than the face of the butting panel (7–8). It helps if a slight space is left between the butting panels to allow for expansion and slight movements in the wall.

Try to finish each corner with a single piece of bead. If the length is such that more than one piece is needed, the butting ends must be cut so they fit

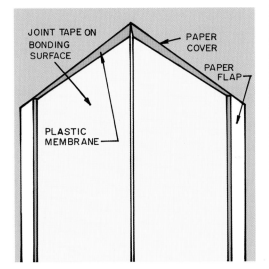

▲ **7-5.** This corner bead has a plastic membrane that is covered with a special paper.

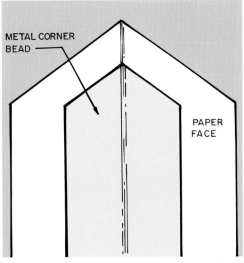

▲ **7-6.** This is a typical paper-faced metal corner bead.

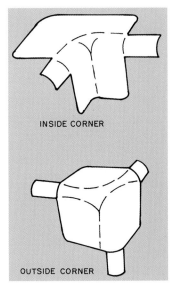

▲ **7-7.** These corner beads make it easy to turn corners.

squarely together. Never overlap the bead at the joint. The beads should be cut so they fit firmly against the ceiling panel and are about ⅜ inch above the floor (7-9).

This allows a little room for expansion, and, if the wall settles, reduces the possibility of a crack forming in the corner. Corner beads are typically available in 8- and 10-foot lengths.

If the corner beads are installed around a wall opening, the front flange is mitered and the back flange is cut square to fit into the opening (7-10). Be certain that all the exposed edges of the gypsum board are filed smooth. Protruding portions will make it impossible to set down the corner bead. Check to see if the opening has been framed square. If it is not, the miter may have to be slightly adjusted. Nail and finish in the normal manner.

INSTALLING VINYL BEADS

Vinyl beads are installed by nailing, bonding with an adhesive, or stapling.

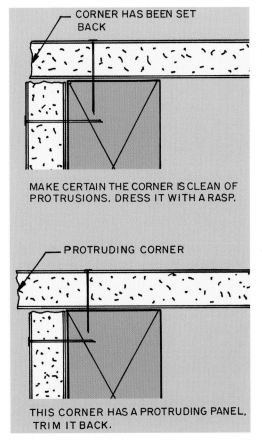

▲ **7-8.** Be certain the panels forming the corner do not extend beyond the butting piece. Consider cutting them a little short.

▲ **7-9.** When possible, each corner bead should be a single piece. It should butt the ceiling panel and be cut ⅜ inch short of the floor.

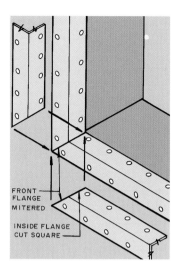

▲ **7–10.** Corner beads installed around openings have the front part of the flange mitered and the part inside the opening cut square.

▲ **7–11.** Place staples in pairs and opposite each other on the flanges.

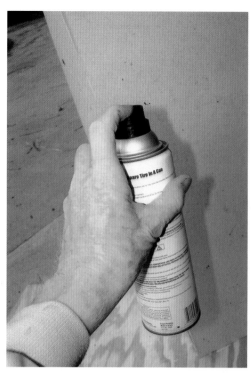

▲ **7–12.** Spray adhesive on the wallboard corner and then on the back of the vinyl bead.

When nailed, 1½- or 1¾-inch drywall nails are driven through the holes every 8 inches. Place them in pairs on each side of the center of the bead. When stapling, use ½-inch staples every 8 inches, spacing one on each side of the center, opposite each other. Place the staples perpendicular to the length of the bead (**7–11**). Manufacturers of vinyl beads supply a spray adhesive for securing the bead to the wallboard. Spray it on the corner and on the back of the bead. Then press the bead in place, starting at the ceiling and working in against the wallboard down to the floor. Some people then staple it to get a superior installation (**7–12**).

If installing bullnose beads, cut the drywall panels a bit short of the corner. This makes room for the curve of the bead to fit against the surface of the panel (**7–13**). They are installed the same as 90-degree beads.

If the corner is not 90 degrees, use flexible splayed corner beads. These are available for inside and outside corners (**7–14**).

Arched openings require the application of a corner bead. The arch bead is cut so it will bend around the opening (**7–15**). It is secured in the same manner as other vinyl beads. After the arch bead has been installed, finish the opening with straight corner bead to the floor. The construction of arches is shown in Chapter 6.

INSTALLING METAL BEADS

Metal beads are usually installed with the same nails used to install the drywall. Place them in the holes in the flanges that are near the outer edges. Place on opposite sides about 8 inches apart (**7–16**). The nails should penetrate the wood framing. Metal corner beads can also be installed with ⁹⁄₁₆-inch staples driven into the gypsum wallboard. They are spaced 12 inches O.C. and opposite each other on the flanges. They are installed perpendicular to the length of the bead. Drywall screws can also be used. Space them every 8 inches.

INSTALLING TRIM AND CORNER BEADS

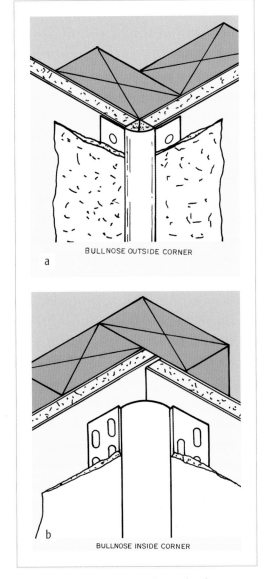

BULLNOSE OUTSIDE CORNER

a

BULLNOSE INSIDE CORNER

b

▲ **7–13.** Bullnose beads give a pleasing rounded corner. Notice the wallboard has been set back to make space for the curve in the outside corner bead.

INSTALLING METAL PAPER-FACED BEADS

Metal paper-faced beads can be installed by laying a thin layer of joint compound on each side of the corner. Some types have a bullnose strip, while others have a square corner. In either case, lay a thin layer of compound on each side of the

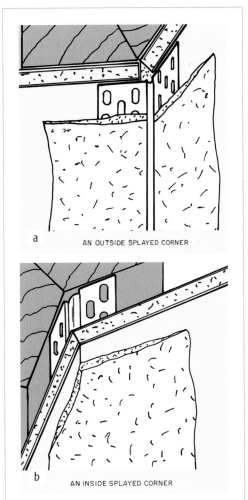

AN OUTSIDE SPLAYED CORNER

a

AN INSIDE SPLAYED CORNER

b

▲ **7–14.** Splayed corner beads are flexible and will adjust to finish inside and outside corners less than and greater than 90 degrees.

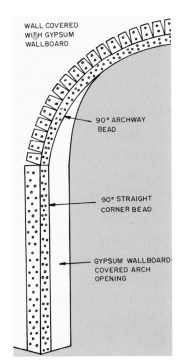

WALL COVERED WITH GYPSUM WALLBOARD

90° ARCHWAY BEAD

90° STRAIGHT CORNER BEAD

GYPSUM WALLBOARD COVERED ARCH OPENING

▲ **7–15.** The corners of arches are covered with archway bead, providing a durable protective edge.

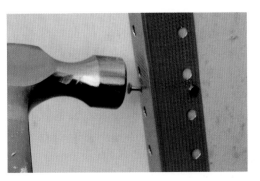

▲ **7–16.** Metal corner beads are installed using drywall nails, screws, or staples. Place them on each side of the bead.

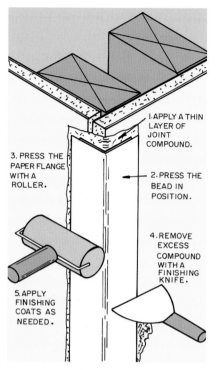

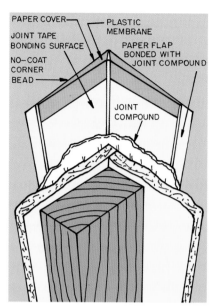

1. APPLY A THIN LAYER OF JOINT COMPOUND.

2. PRESS THE BEAD IN POSITION.

3. PRESS THE PAPER FLANGE WITH A ROLLER.

4. REMOVE EXCESS COMPOUND WITH A FINISHING KNIFE.

5. APPLY FINISHING COATS AS NEEDED.

▲ **7–17.** Metal paper-faced corner beads are bonded to the wallboard with joint cement.

PAPER COVER

JOINT TAPE BONDING SURFACE

NO–COAT CORNER BEAD

PLASTIC MEMBRANE

PAPER FLAP BONDED WITH JOINT COMPOUND

JOINT COMPOUND

▲ **7–18.** The No-Coat bead is bonded to the drywall by a thin layer of joint compound that bonds the special joint tape on the back to the drywall. *(Courtesy Structus Building Technologies, Inc.)*

▲ **7–19.** After the joint compound has been sprayed on the corner, the bead is applied using a manufacturer-supplied drywall corner bead box. *(Courtesy Structus Building Technologies, Inc.).*

corner. Place the bead in position and press the paper flange into the compound with a special roller. Excess compound is then carefully removed with a taping knife (**7–17**). After the compound has hardened, several finishing coats can be applied over the paper surface.

INSTALLING PLASTIC PAPER-FACED BEADS

The plastic paper-faced bead system is referred to as the No Coat system because it only requires a single light finishing coat. The corner bead is installed by bonding it to the drywall with a thin coat of joint compound (**7–18**). Two methods of applying the compound are available. One uses a manufacturer-supplied compound hopper. The bead is fed through the hopper, which coats it with a thin layer of compound. The coated strip is then pressed in place on the corner. The other tool works from a canister of compound, which is under pressure. It sprays the required amount and width on the corner. The bead is then pressed against the wallboard. This is made easier by using bead from a special drywall corner bead box (**7–19**).

After the bead is in place, it is rolled with special tools to seat it against the drywall. In **7–20**, an exterior corner is being pressed in place. The rollers can be adjusted for use on interior corners. Long, flat runs are sealed with rollers, as shown in **7–21**. Notice in **7–20** that some of the compound has squeezed out along the edge of the paper flap. This is removed by moving a taping knife along the seam.

Finally, a thin finishing coat of joint compound is run along each side of the bead. The tool in **7–22** lays the correct width and thickness in a single pass.

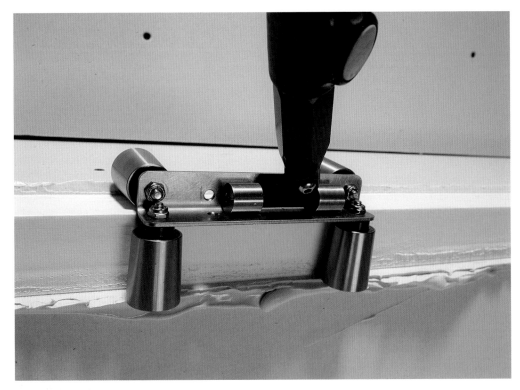

▼ **7–20.** After the bead is pressed against the drywall, it is firmly bonded by pressing it in place against the drywall with a special roller tool. *(Courtesy Structus Building Technologies, Inc.)*

▲ **7–21.** Flat beads are rolled in place with special roller tools. *(Courtesy Structus Building Technologies, Inc.)*

▲ **7–22.** After the bead is firmly in place, a thin finish coat is applied over each side with a special compound applicator. *(Courtesy Structus Building Technologies, Inc.)*

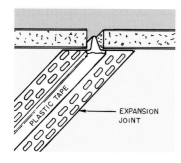

EXPANSION JOINT

▲ **7–23.** An expansion joint before the flanges are finished with drywall compound.

INSTALLING J-BEADS

Sometimes the end of a panel is exposed, such as might occur at an opening or at the ceiling where you choose not to tape the joint. J-beads are used to finish these edges (refer to **7–1**, or page 77). This bead may be metal or vinyl. It is placed over the edge of the gypsum panel and is held in place without nails. A thin coat of adhesive could be applied to the back, bonding it to the wood or metal framing, but this is not required.

Expansion Joints

Expansion joints are installed when the size of the area covered by drywall exceeds 30 feet in length or whenever the ceiling is longer than 50 feet or has a total area of 2,500 square feet or more. They are secured in the same manner as corner beads. A typical installation is shown in **7–23**. Additional information is given in Chapter 10.

Finishing Drywall PART III

Finishing Tools and Materials

8

AFTER THE DRYWALL PANELS *are securely in place, it is time to begin the finishing process, which includes concealing the nails and screws, covering the joints between the panels, and finishing the corner beads. The materials used for this type of work include joint compound and reinforcing tape.*

Joint Compounds

Joint compounds serve three basic functions:

1. To bond the joint tape over a joint in the wallboard and serve as a finish coating over the tape, corner beads, and screw and nail heads, or to bond panels that are laminated;
2. To produce a textured finish on the wallboard;
3. To laminate wallboard to another wall finish material such as gypsum wallboard, old plaster surfaces, or backer-board surfaces;

There are a number of different types of joint compounds available. Manufacturers' brochures list each type they can supply and give specific values and uses. Basically, they fall into two classifications: drying-type and setting type. They are available in powder form (water is added, and the compound is mixed with a power mixer) and premixed ready-to-use products. Premixed compound is available in 1-gallon and 5-gallon buckets (**8–1**). The advantage of pre-mixed is that the consistency has been established by the manufacturer and is consistent from bucket to bucket. It is ready to use with no additional reparation.

▶ **8–1.** This is a widely used premixed all-purpose joint compound.

Powdered compound has the same basic properties as pre-mixed; however, it requires that carefully measured quantities of water be added and the mixture be thoroughly stirred. Typically, it is mixed with a mud mixer installed in a powerful electric drill (8–2), but hand mixers are also available.

Following are descriptions of many of the types of joint compounds currently available. Consult your building supply dealer for additional information.

DRYING-TYPE JOINT COMPOUNDS

Drying-type joint compounds are vinyl-based and harden as the water evaporates. They can be used for all of the various finishing procedures.

Drying-type joint compounds should not be applied if the temperature of the air and wallboard and the compound is less that 44°F. The compound must be thoroughly dry before the next coat is applied. Drying time will vary due to the temperature, ventilation of the area, and the humidity. Typically, at least 24 hours of drying is needed.

All-purpose joint compounds are used to install tape, finish corners, and for spotting, final finish, texturing, laminating, or skim coating. They are good for repairs. Two types are available, one for hand application and a thinner type for mechanical tool application. All-purpose compound is not as strong as topping and taping compound, and it doesn't have the latter's bonding properties.

Lightweight joint compounds serve the same purposes as all-purpose joint compounds, but are lighter, easier to sand, and have less shrinkage. They are

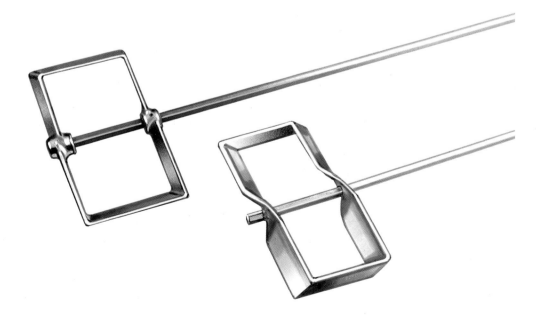

▶ **8–2.** Powdered joint compound is mixed with water using mixers like these rotated by a powerful electric drill.
(Courtesy Kraft Tool Company)

typically 35 percent lighter than all-purpose compound.

Taping compounds are designed especially for bonding tape, corner beads, and laminating wallboard. They provide a better bond than all-purpose compounds.

Topping compounds are designed for use as the finish coat over the joint compound used to bond the tape, corner bead, and cover nail and screw heads. They have excellent sanding properties and can be used for texturing.

Texture-grade compounds are formulated to be used to spray on walls and ceilings, providing a rough, textured finish. Typical finishes include sprayed spatter, knockdown, skip towel, and orange peel.

DUST-CONTROL COMPOUNDS

There is a lightweight joint compound that is formulated to provide some control over the dust created by sanding. This compound creates the same amount of dust particles as regular compound; however, the particles clump together as they fall to the floor, forming piles that are bonded and easier to clean away than unbonded dust particles.

SETTING COMPOUNDS

Setting compounds harden by a chemical reaction. They are available in powdered and premixed form. They are available in a range of drying times, typically from 20 minutes to several hours. Compounds with quicker drying times mean less time to lay the coat, but the next coat can be applied sooner. This type is more difficult to smooth by sanding, so extra care is needed when applying to get it as smooth as possible. Some types are not affected by humidity after they have hardened, and are used when taping moisture-resistant wallboard or in areas that may develop humidity above normal.

STORING JOINT COMPOUND

Typically, joint compound can be stored up to six months if kept in normal temperatures and tightly sealed containers. Protect it from extreme heat or cold. If it freezes, allow it to thaw at room temperatures for 24 to 48 hours.

Reinforcing Tape

Reinforcing tape is applied over the joints between panels and is used to repair damaged areas. It is placed in the first layer of joint compound. This helps cover the joint and reinforces the compound, so it is less likely to crack. Tape is used on all joints between the edges and ends of panels and to reinforce inside corners. Special tapes are available for use on cement board.

PAPER TAPE

Paper tape is most commonly used. You will find that it is easy to handle and that it works into the joint compound with a few strokes of the taping knife. The tape has a slightly rough surface to increase the bond with the joint compound. Some types have small perforations to increase bonding strength. The tape has a crease run down the center, making it easy to fold for use on inside corners.

Paper tape is available in $1^{31}/_{32}$- and $2\,^1/_{16}$-inch widths, and is sold in 75-, 250-, and 500-foot rolls (**8–3**). It takes about 370 lineal feet to tape 1,000 square feet of drywall.

FIBERGLASS JOINT TAPE

Fiberglass joint tape is made by weaving high-strength glass fibers, which form an open mesh (**8–4**). It is available with a non-adhesive back, and is usually stapled to the drywall. It is also available with an adhesive back; this type is bonded to the

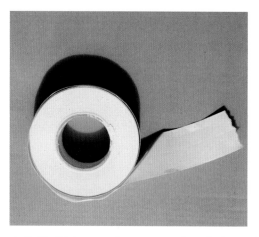

▲ **8–3.** High-strength paper tape is typically used to cover the joints between the drywall panels. When finished with several topping coats, it provides a strong covering.

▲ **8–4.** Fiberglass tape has a coarse open mesh and is available with an adhesive back or non-adhesive back.

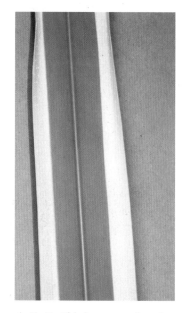

▲ **8–5.** This is a paper-faced metal corner bead. The metal line and the covering paper face are bonded to the wallboard with joint cement.

drywall by pressing it in place with a drywall knife. Run the knife firmly along the entire length of the tape. Then lay the joint compound over it. Some manufacturers recommend using a setting-type compound for the first coat. For additional coats, use either a setting-type or a drying-type. Fiberglass tape is especially useful in repairing small, damaged areas, and all-purpose compound can be used in these areas.

PREFINISHED CORNER TAPE

Prefinished corner tape is used to finish inside and outside corners. After installation, it does not require the several coats of drywall compound as does paper tape. It is ready to paint with no additional preparation. One such product, No-Coat Ultraflex, is a laminate consisting of a paper-back ply, a copolymer in the center, and a paperboard front layer. It is 4¼ inches wide, and has a molded center hinge to facilitate forming the corner.

PAPER-FACED METAL CORNER BEADS

These are a combination of laminated paper joint tape and metal strips. They are recommended for use on inside corners or archways, drop ceilings, cathedral ceilings, kneewalls, stairways, or any inside or outside corner less or greater than 90 degrees. They are applied with the metal side to the face of the wallboard, and are embedded into the joint compound (8–5).

Corner Beads

External corners are reinforced with metal or vinyl corner beads (8–6). Since these corners are very likely to get bumped while the room is in use, the extra strength is needed. Paper tape will not yield the corner that's needed for the long run. Some applications can be seen in Chapter 7. The flanges on the beads are nailed through the gypsum into the stud. Notice they are heavily perforated. This helps the joint compound to bond to them. The flexible metal tape in 8–3 is also used for corner beads.

FINISHING TOOLS AND MATERIALS

Metal Trim

Metal trim is used to provide protection and neat finished edges to gypsum panels where they meet doors and windows, or intersect with panels made from other materials. (You can see some examples in Chapter 7.) Dry wall manufacturers offer quite a variety of trim shapes for use on wood- and steel-framed buildings.

Finishing Tools

Possibly the most important finishing tool is a set of **high-quality taping and finishing knives**. The best have steel blades, but plastic-bladed knives are also available. Gaining experience with them is about the only way to see which you prefer.

You will need a **6-inch joint taping knife** that is used to apply the filler coats of joint compound over the nail, screws, and joints (8–7) as well as **8-, 10-, and 12-inch finishing knives** for spreading the finish coats over the tape coat (8–8).

Finishing trowels are often used to dress the final finishing coats on joints requiring a wide strip of finishing compound (8–9).

Some drywall finishers like to use a corner joint finishing trowel (8–10). Using this trowel speeds up taping the corner because it can smooth both sides with only one stroke.

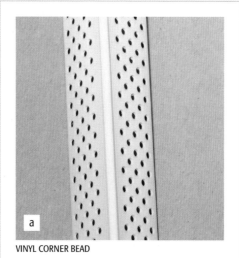

VINYL CORNER BEAD

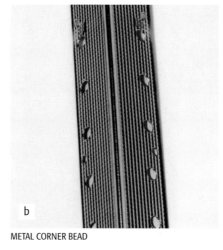

METAL CORNER BEAD

▲ **8–6.** Typical vinyl and metal corner beads.

▲ **8–7.** Joint taping knives are available in 4-, 5-, and 6-inch-wide blades. *(Courtesy The Stanley Works).*

▲ **8–8.** Finishing knives are available in widths from 6 to 14 inches. *(Courtesy Kraft Tool Company)*

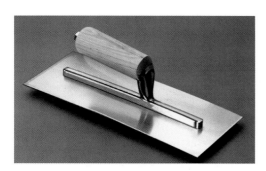

▲ **8–9.** Drywall trowels have stainless-steel blades that range in length from 12 to 16 inches. *(Courtesy Kraft Tool Company)*

▲ **8–10.** These inside and outside corner tools smooth both sides of the corner with one pass. *(Courtesy Kraft Tool Company)*

▲ **8–11** Flexible rubber taping and wipe-down knives are designed for finishing inside and outside corners. *(Courtesy Kraft Tool Company)*

Flexible rubber taping knives for inside and outside corners are also available (**8–11**). The blade is adjustable to allow the flexibility needed for finishing corners.

A **mud pan** is needed to hold the joint compound, and the **tape knife** moves the compound from the pan to the wall (**8–12**).

The **mud holder** in **8–13** is carried by the taper. It stores a limited amount of compound for immediate use.

Excess compound on the walls and ceiling can be scraped away with the wall scraper in **8–14**.

Some type of **tin snips** or **aviation snips** are needed to cut the metal and plastic beads and trim. Many finishers seem to prefer aviation snips (**8–15**).

Sanding Tools

Tools used for sanding include a hand sander, pole sander, sanding sponges, sanding screens, and carbide sandpaper.

The **hand sander** is about 3×9 inches in size. It has clamps on each end to hold the sanding abrasive material (**8–16**).

A **pole sander** has a flat pad connected to a long pole, letting you reach the top of the wall, and, in some cases, the ceiling from the floor (**8–17**).

A **commercial sanding machine** with a wet/dry vacuum greatly reduces the dust in the air (**8–18**).

Sanding screens are carbide-grit-coated fiberglass mesh. Both sides are abrasive-coated and can be used until they wear out. The screen (mesh) has

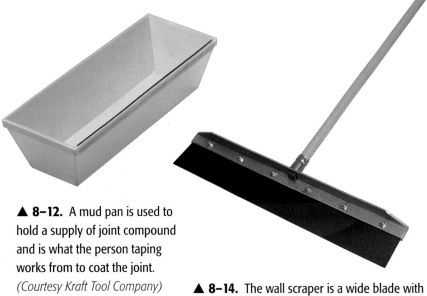

▲ **8–12.** A mud pan is used to hold a supply of joint compound and is what the person taping works from to coat the joint. *(Courtesy Kraft Tool Company)*

▲ **8–14.** The wall scraper is a wide blade with a long handle. It is used to scrape excess compound from walls and ceilings. *(Courtesy Kraft Tool Company)*

▶ **8–13.** The drywall mud holder is held by the finisher and holds a small supply of joint compound for immediate use. *(Courtesy Kraft Tool Company)*

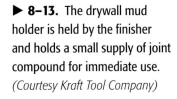

▲ **8–15.** Tin snips can be used to cut metal corner bead. *(Courtesy Kraft Tool Company)*

▲ **8–16.** This hand sander has a comfortable handle, is made from lightweight aluminum, and has clamps that hold the abrasive paper against the rubber bottom. *(Courtesy Kraft Tool Company)*

FINISHING TOOLS AND MATERIALS

holes due to the mesh, which enable the dust to fall through and thus not clog the surface. Screens are available in degrees of coarseness from 120 to 200. The larger the grit number, the finer the abrasive. Sanding screens cost more than drywall sandpaper but last longer and cut faster (8–19).

Drywall sanding paper has a tough paper backing with a black carbide-grit surface. It is available in 80, 100, 120, 150 grit. The higher the grit number, the finer the abrasive. The fine abrasives are used for the final finish sanding. The coarser grits are used for the first sanding, to remove excess compound rapidly.

Sanding sponges are used if you decide to wet-sand the compound. Made of a high-density polyurethane, they have a soft, nonabrasive surface. They are wetted and used to lightly blend in the feathered edges. They are not used on ridges, lumps, or other larger defects that need smoothing.

◄ **8–17.** A pole sander has an aluminum base with a rubber pad upon which the sandpaper is clamped, and a long pole connected to the pad with a swivel. *(Courtesy Kraft Tool Company)*

Dust Protection

Some form of respiratory protection is vital when sanding drywall and applying spray-on textures. Not all masks and respirators can be used for all types of air contaminants. There is a cheap dust mask that looks like the one shown in 8–20 but is not NIOSH-approved. (NIOSH is the National Institute for Occupational Safety and Health.) Before

◄ **8–18.** This drywall power sander has a sanding head connected to a vacuum that pulls most of the gypsum dust out of the air. *(Courtesy Porter-Cable)*

PRECUT DRYWALL
SANDPAPER

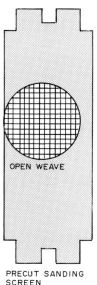

OPEN WEAVE

PRECUT SANDING
SCREEN

▲ **8–19.** Drywall sandpaper and sanding screens are sold precut to fit hand and pole sanders.

buying any type of mask, read the label to be certain it is approved for use when sanding drywall.

Good-quality goggles are also necessary to keep your eyes from dust (**8–21**). Overhead sanding is a special problem when you must avoid dust in your face and hair. The full face mask shown in **8–22** will provide excellent protection.

Sanding also tends to let gypsum dust filter into adjoining rooms. Dust doors can be installed on all openings to contain the dust in the room being sanded. One type is shown in **8–23**.

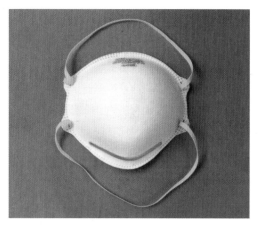

▲ **8–20.** This dust mask is NIOSH-approved for use when sanding drywall. There are dust masks that look similar but are not approved and should not be used.

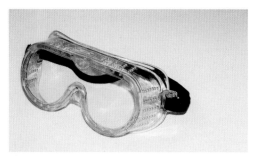

▲ **8–21.** Tight-fitting goggles are needed to protect your eyes from sanding dust and other sources of injury. *(Courtesy Kraft Tool Company)*

▲ **8–22.** A full face mask will provide excellent protection when sanding and installing panels overhead.

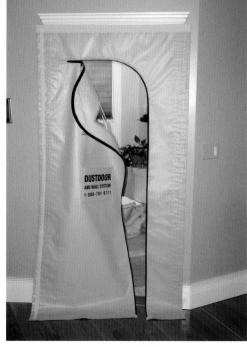

▲ **8–23.** Plastic dust doors will keep the sanding dust within the room. *(Courtesy Brophy Design, Inc.)*

Finding and Correcting Defects

9

MANY PROBLEMS THAT MAY *affect the final quality of the finished wall can be present well before the drywall installers begin their work. Defects can be introduced as the carpenter frames the walls and ceilings. These problems need to be caught and corrected before the drywall process begins. The general contractor should be informed about framing problems so that the proper workers can return to the site and make corrections. In addition to framing, the electrical, plumbing, insulation, and mechanical contractors need to do their jobs correctly. Following are some things to look for and possible corrections.*

Panel Damage

Before installing gypsum drywall, check to be certain that the material you have is in good condition. Improper handling and storage can render gypsum wallboard panels useless or at least in need of some remedial repair action. Following are things you should check.

DAMAGED EDGES

Improper handling may result in damaged edges and broken corners to the gypsum drywall. This type of damage tears the paper and crushes the core. Before using these panels, cut off the damaged section.

WATER DAMAGE

If the panels get wet, it is possible that the paper will come loose from the gypsum and the gypsum core may even soften. Dry those panels that seem to still have the paper glue bond intact and a hard core. If greater damage has occurred, discard the panel.

MILDEW

Panels stored under moist conditions or that have accidentally been wet will tend to have a growth of mildew. This can be prevented by storing panels in a dry area. However, if you end up with mildewed

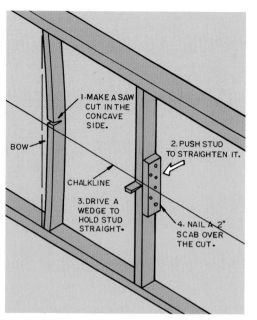

1. MAKE A SAW CUT IN THE CONCAVE SIDE.

BOW

2. PUSH STUD TO STRAIGHTEN IT.

CHALKLINE

3. DRIVE A WEDGE TO HOLD STUD STRAIGHT.

4. NAIL A 2" SCAB OVER THE CUT.

▲ **9–1.** Run a chalkline to check for bowed studs. Straighten those slightly bowed by driving a wood wedge in a saw cut made in the concave side of the bow and then nailing a 2-inch scab over the cut. Often it is best to replace the stud.

panels, then separate them and carefully clean the paper with a mix of 1 cup of bleach and 3 cups of water. Do not scrub hard enough to damage the paper. Place the panels flat with wood strips between each so air can circulate to dry them.

Framing Problems

Many of the problems that occur when installing drywall or that occur some time after the job is finished are due to framing defects.

BOWED STUDS

Before starting to install the drywall, check the studs and ceiling joists to be certain they are in the same plane. Run a chalkline down the wall or ceiling joists. This quickly shows if something is out of line. If a stud is bowed, it can be straightened by cutting into the concave side of

the bow and driving a wedge into the cut (**9–1**). This wedging will correct small bows. Generally, the best solution is to replace the stud.

STUDS OUT OF ALIGNMENT

This often occurs when a stud is not placed flush on the bottom or top plate (see Chapter 5 for nailing problems). When gypsum wallboard is nailed to this stud, the nails will puncture through the panel or the panel will fracture with the hammer blow. If the misalignment is small (⅛ inch), remove problem fasteners and only nail at a place where the panel touches the stud.

THE FRAME PROTRUDES BEYOND THE STUDS

As shown in Chapter 5, parts of the framing—such as fire stops between studs or bridging between floor joists—occasionally extend beyond the stud. This holds the gypsum panel out from the wall. The wallboard will not fit tight and nails will generally tear through the paper and even fracture the gypsum core. These defected framing elements must be made flush with the studs or joists before drywall installation starts.

TWISTED FRAMING MEMBERS

Any time a framing member, such as a stud, is not nailed square, some part of it will protrude beyond the line of the wall (see Chapter 5). Also, the same thing can result from using warped stock. Straightened framing members should be straightened before installing the drywall. Warped members, however, should be replaced. If the warping (due to improperly dried lumber) occurs after the wall is finished, do not bother to make repairs until the house has gone through one heating season. When you think they have stabilized, remove the problem fasteners and replace with screws. Drive them carefully so you do not crush the core.

Defects Due to Fasteners

Possibly the most common defect in a drywall installation is improper nailing. It is well worth your time to slow down just a little and get each fastener in straight and with the proper degree of tightness. These are the major cause of nail pops.

NAIL POPS

Nail pop refers to when the head of a nail pops through the face of the joint compound, creating a defect (9–2). This is caused by many of the problems just mentioned: stress, improperly driven nails, and loose panels. The major cause of pops is lumber shrinkage. Pops occurring several months after the walls have been completed are usually due to lumber shrinkage (9–3). To correct a nail pop, remove any loose gypsum and torn paper from around the fastener, press the panel against the framing, and set the nail against the panel in a dimple so it is a little below the surface (9–4). Do not break the gypsum core. Then drive nails, or better still, screws 1½ inches above and below the popped nail. Then cover the fasteners with joint cement. The electric screwdriver in 9–5 quickly drives screws and produces the proper dimple. Very small holes, such as those of ¼- to ½-inch diameters, can be repaired using the same coating procedure.

DEPRESSED NAILS

Nails that are dimpled too deeply or driven when framing defects have not been corrected typically break the paper on the panel. This is sometimes caused when too few nails are used and the weight of the panel tends to pull them

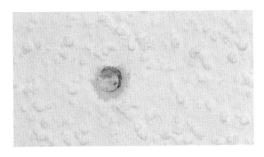

▲ **9–2.** Nail pops produce an unsightly spot on the panel. They are usually due to improper installation.

through the surface. Remove the depressed nails if this can be done without breaking the gypsum core. Then renail the entire panel. Consider double-nailing as an extra precaution. (See Chapter 5 for more on nailing problems.)

RUPTURING THE FACE PAPER

There are any number of reasons why the face paper may be broken. Carelessly driven nails, dimples that are too deep, or improper framing are common causes. Sometimes the panel is not held tight to the framing and a hammer blow will break the paper. Often, when the face paper is ruptured, the core is also broken. This gives the panel almost no support.

Remove the faulty nails and then renail. Be sure to keep the wallboard tight to the framing and drive the nail straight. Be careful to set the head in a very shallow dimple.

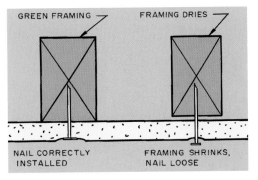

GREEN FRAMING — FRAMING DRIES —

NAIL CORRECTLY INSTALLED — FRAMING SHRINKS, NAIL LOOSE

◀ **9–3.** Green studs shrink as they dry, producing a loose panel that can cause the nail to pop through the gypsum coating.

▶ 9–4. How to repair a popped nail:

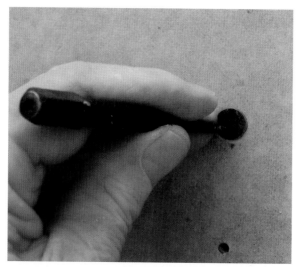

1. AFTER REMOVING LOOSE GYPSUM AND PAPER AROUND THE POPPED NAIL, PRESS THE PANEL AGAINST THE FRAMING AND CAREFULLY SET THE NAIL BELOW THE SURFACE OF THE PANEL.

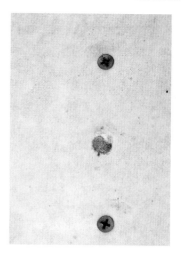

2. DRIVE NAILS OR DRYWALL SCREWS 1½ INCHES ABOVE AND BELOW THE POPPED FASTENER. SET THE SCREWHEAD JUST A LITTLE BELOW THE SURFACE OF THE PANEL, BUT DO NOT BREAK THE GYPSUM CORE.

3. COVER THE FASTENERS WITH JOINT COMPOUND. USE SEVERAL COATS AS NEEDED.

FINDING AND CORRECTING DEFECTS

▲ 9–5. This electric automatic screwdriver will rapidly deliver screws, install them, and produce the proper dimple for covering the screw. *(Courtesy Pam Fastening Technology, Inc.)*

POUNDING

Sometimes when the second side of a wall is being nailed, the pounding can jar and loosen the nails on the other side. If you hold the panel tight when nailing, this is less likely to happen. After both sides have been nailed, carefully go over those that are loose to reset and dimple them. If screws or adhesive are used, the panels are less likely to come loose. You may want to double-nail close to a loose nail in a single-nail application.

LOOSE SCREWS

Since screw guns can be adjusted to the proper torque, it is not likely that loose screws will occur. However, if the gun is not set properly or the wallboard is not held firmly against the wall, this can occur. Recheck for loose screws and reset them with a screw gun that has been properly adjusted.

LOOSE PANELS

Loose panels are caused when the fasteners are driven and the panels are not held tight against the framing. Before giving the nail or screw its final setting, press the panel firmly against the framing.

BULGES AROUND FASTENERS

Bulges can occur around a fastener if it is driven too deep, the wrong tool is used, or the facing paper and core are damaged by a loosely installed panel.

When joint cement is placed over this damaged area, it tends to swell, creating an unwanted bulge. If possible, remove the improperly driven fastener, drive one or more screws on each side, and clean out the damaged core and loose paper. Then coat with joint compound.

Improper Panel Fits

If a panel is a bit too long and you try to force it between two panels or a panel and framing, it will tend to bow (**9–6**). It will not have firm contact with the framing. It is not possible to properly nail this panel, and nail pops or a crushed panel core are certain to occur. Always cut the panel a bit shorter than the space to be covered. Panels that have already been installed-but are too long-must be removed and new ones set in place.

▼ 9–6. Gypsum panels that are too long will tend to bow, producing nail pops. *(Courtesy United States Gypsum Corporation).*

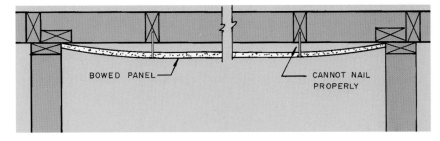

Sagging Panels

Ceiling panels can begin to sag some months after installation because of the excessive weight of insulation or a textured ceiling, or due to excessive humidity or wetting from some other cause. Using panels that are too thin or not designed for use on the ceiling will eventually lead to sag.

To correct, remove the panel, replace with panels of the proper thickness, and double-nail. Consider using high-strength gypsum ceiling panels designed to resist sag. The ceiling can be furred down and completely recovered. In any case, the weight causing the sag must be addressed in some way to prevent a recurrence.

Repairing Holes

Occasionally during construction and often after the building is occupied, the gypsum wallboard will receive a blow that fractures the surface, causing a hole. There are a number of ways these can be repaired. Possibly the easiest way for the home-owner to repair a ruptured spot is to buy a repair kit at the local building supply store.

CHOOSING A JOINT COMPOUND

Consider using 20- to 30-minute setting compound for filling any holes and for the first taping coat. It hardens much faster that general-purpose joint compound, so you can apply the first taping coat as soon as the first coat with the tape hardens.

If you use the powdered type, mix only what you can use immediately. Since it hardens rapidly, you will need to quickly clean the mud pan and taping knife. Do not scrape the old compound into a sink, as it will clog the drain.

Consider using fiberglass mesh tape. The adhesive type will eliminate the need to lay on a thin layer of compound to hold the tape in place. Use the cross-fiber mesh type because it adds strength and crack resistance to the repair patch. The non-adhesive fiberglass mesh is installed over the joint with staples.

One variety of repair kit uses metal clips that are secured to the edges of the opening after cutting them straight and clean (9–7). Cut a square or rectangular opening, and install the clips. Cut a gypsum wallboard patch to fit the opening. Screw through the patch into the clip, and finish the joints in a normal manner (9–8).

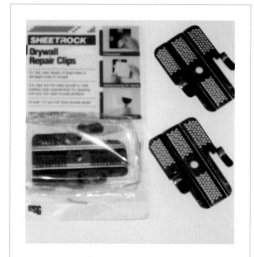

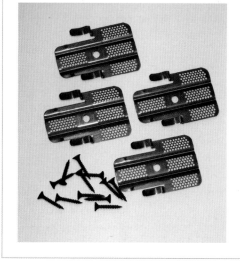

▲ **9–7.** A metal clip is used to hold the repair patches in holes in gypsum drywall.

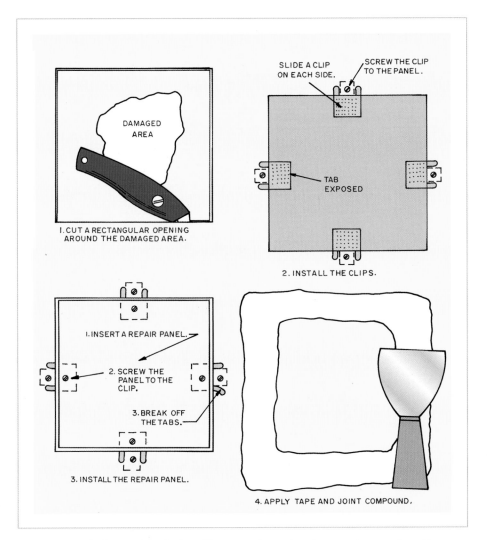

DAMAGED AREA

1. CUT A RECTANGULAR OPENING AROUND THE DAMAGED AREA.

SLIDE A CLIP ON EACH SIDE.

SCREW THE CLIP TO THE PANEL.

TAB EXPOSED

2. INSTALL THE CLIPS.

1. INSERT A REPAIR PANEL.

2. SCREW THE PANEL TO THE CLIP.

3. BREAK OFF THE TABS.

3. INSTALL THE REPAIR PANEL.

4. APPLY TAPE AND JOINT COMPOUND.

▲ **9–8.** A typical procedure for installing a repair patch, using metal supporting clips.

Another product has a fiberglass mesh tape bonded to an aluminum backing. Make the repair by removing any loose core material and face paper around the damaged area. Then press the adhesive-backed aluminum over the hole (**9–9**). Apply a coat of joint compound over the entire patch. When it is dry, sand it and apply additional coats as needed. After the final coat, lightly sand to a smooth surface.

If you are in a hurry as you make repairs, consider using a setting compound for the final coats. Depending upon the setting time of the compound you choose, you can put on several coats in a few hours.

Another repair procedure is shown in **9–10**. Mark a rectangular section around the damage and cut on this line on a 45-degree angle. Smooth the edges of these cuts on the sides of the opening. Then cut a patch from a piece of scrap. The patch has 45-degree bevels facing the back paper. It must be cut and smoothed to fit exactly in the wall opening. Apply joint compound to the beveled sides of the wall opening and set

▶ **9-9.** Small holes can be repaired by using an adhesive-backed fiberglass mesh patch that is covered with joint compound in the normal manner.

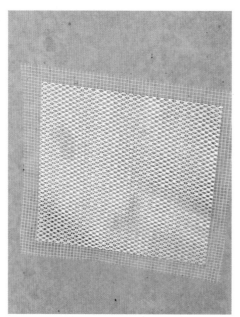

1. PLACE THE ADHESIVE BACK OF THE FIBERGLASS PATCH OVER THE DAMAGED AREA. PRESS FIRMLY AGAINST THE WALLBOARD.

2. APPLY A LAYER OF JOINT COMPOUND OVER THE PATCH, WORKING IT INTO THE OPENINGS IN THE MESH. AFTER IT DRIES, APPLY TWO OR THREE ADDITIONAL COATS IN THE NORMAL MANNER. FEATHER EACH COAT OUT AROUND THE PATCH TO GIVE A SMOOTH FLOW OVER THE WALLBOARD.

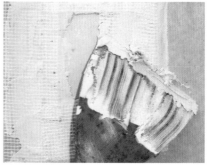

1. CUT A BEVELED RECTANGULAR OPENING AROUND THE DAMAGED AREAS AND CUT A PATCH FROM DRYWALL WITH THE EDGES BEVELED TOWARD THE BACK.

2. PLACE JOINT COMPOUND ON THE SIDES OF THE OPENING.

3. PRESS THE PATCH INTO THE OPENING.

4. LAY A LAYER OF JOINT COMPOUND AROUND THE SIDES AND PRESS THE FIBERGLASS TAPE INTO IT AND SMOOTH THE COMPOUND. WHEN IT HAS SET, APPLY TWO OR THREE ADDITIONAL COATS IN THE NORMAL MANNER.

▲ **9-10.** This patch requires the edges of the opening and the drywall to be beveled.

the patch in place. Then tape the joint edges in the normal manner.

A repair of a fairly large hole can be made by installing wood backup strips, as shown in **9-11**. Install the wood strips with screws. Then cut a patch close to the shape of the opening. Fasten it to the wood strips with screws. Fill the gaps between the patch and wallboard with joint compound and then cover the joint with tape and compound.

FINDING AND CORRECTING DEFECTS

ENCLOSING LARGE OPENINGS

If the damaged area is rather large, it is best to cut the drywall away, leaving an opening from stud to stud. This same technique is used when you want to cover a window or door opening that is to be closed. If it is a major remodeling job and several openings are involved, some people prefer to strip the wall and cover it with new drywall panels. However, just the opening can be covered by framing it with 2 × 3 members (**9–12**), and then cutting a piece of drywall to fit into the opening, leaving a ³⁄₁₆-inch space on all sides. Screw or nail it to the framing. Then lay mesh tape over the edges and bond it with drywall

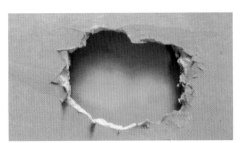

1. A SMALL BUT SERIOUSLY DAMAGED SPOT.

2. CUT A DRYWALL PATCH ABOUT TWO INCHES WIDER AND LONGER THAN THE DAMAGE. PLACE IT OVER THE HOLE AND MARK AROUND IT.

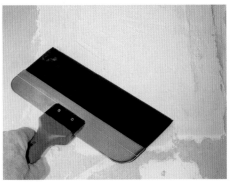

3. CUT THE RECTANGULAR AREA FOR THE PATCH. IT CAN BE CUT WITH A UTILITY KNIFE, SMALL HACKSAW, DRYWALL KEYHOLE SAW, OR SABER SAW.

4. INSTALL ONE-INCH-THICK WOOD STRIPS ON EACH SIDE OF THE OPENING WITH SCREWS RUN THROUGH THE DRYWALL.

5. TRIM THE PATCH TO FIT, LEAVING A ⅛-INCH SPACE AROUND THE EDGES. SCREW IT TO THE WOOD STRIPS. THEN COVER THE EDGES WITH FIBERGLASS MESH TAPE AND JOINT COMPOUND.

6. WHEN THE PATCH IS DRY, APPLY ADDITIONAL COATS OF COMPOUND AS NEEDED, COVERING THE ENTIRE PATCH AND FEATHERING OUT THE EDGES.

◄ **9–11.** This drywall patch is screwed to wood strips that are secured to the drywall at the edges of the opening. Then tape and finish the edges in the normal manner.

1. WHEN A LARGE AREA IS TO BE COVERED, CUT THE DRYWALL FROM STUD TO STUD. BUILD A FRAME OF 2 × 4-INCH WOOD FRAMING INSIDE THE OPENING.

2. IF THE OPENING IS ON AN EXTERIOR WALL, REMEMBER TO ADD INSULATION AND COVER IT WITH A VAPOR BARRIER ON THE ROOM SIDE.

3. CUT A DRYWALL PANEL TO FIT INTO THE OPENING. SCREW OR NAIL IT TO THE 2 × 4 FRAME.

4. COVER THE EDGES WITH FIBERGLASS MESH TAPE AND FINISH WITH JOINT COMPOUND IN THE NORMAL MANNER.

▲ **9–12.** For large wall openings that need covering, cut the existing drywall back to the nearest studs. Then frame this opening with 2 × 4-inch wood pieces. Finally, install a new gypsum panel over the opening.

compound. When it is dry, apply three or four finish nails over the entire patch and feather it out on the wall about 12 inches. This will help the thickened wall area flow smoothly into the surrounding wall surface.

Joint Problems

The visible defects on a finished panel occur at the taped joints or the heads of

fasteners. Proper installation over adequate framing will reduce these defects to a minimum. Bonding the panels to the framing with adhesive and using screws instead of nails will also help. Following are repairs for some joint problems.

After the tape has been installed and the joint compound has dried, blisters may occur. These are caused by using too thin a coat of joint compound under the tape, not pressing the tape firmly into the compound, or pressing the tape too hard against the wallboard, which squeezes out too much compound.

To repair a blister in the tape, slit each blister with a knife and remove any dried compound below it. Then lay compound beneath the tape and smooth it flat. The compound should bond it in place. Finish by laying a skim coat of compound over it. Let this dry before applying additional finish coats. It may be necessary to scrape out some of the dried compound beneath the tape so the surface is smooth and clean.

EDGE CRACKING

Sometimes long, narrow cracks will appear along the edges of the tape. Many things can cause this to happen. It could be caused by drying at too high a temperature (which causes rapid drying); using the wrong joint compound or one that has been diluted too much; leaving too much joint compound under the tape; or wet or cold conditions at the time of application that resulted in reduced bonding between the tape and paper on the panel.

To correct this defect, cut away any poorly bonded sections of tape. Cover these hairline cracks with a two- or three-pound cut shellac, and cut a groove into any wide cracks and coat with shellac. Once the shellac has dried, recoat with joint compound and a new layer of tape.

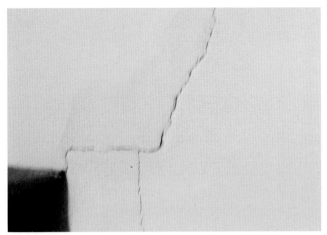

1 CRACKS FREQUENTLY OCCUR AT THE CORNERS OF OPENINGS IN THE WALL.

2. CUT THE CRACK WIDER IN A V-SHAPE. SOME PEOPLE PREFER TO MAKE IT WIDER AT THE BOTTOM TO HELP HOLD THE FILLING COMPOUND IN THE CRACK.

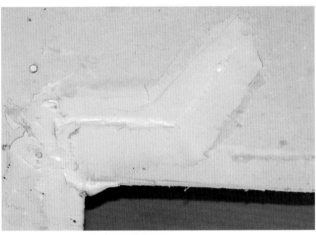

3 FILL THE V-GROOVE WITH JOINT COMPOUND.

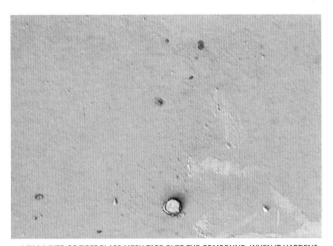

4. LAY A LAYER OF FIBERGLASS MESH TAPE OVER THE COMPOUND. WHEN IT HARDENS, ADD ADDITIONAL COATS OF COMPOUND IN THE NORMAL MANNER.

▲ **9–13.** Stress cracks must be stabilized before filling and taping.

CRACKS IN THE CENTER OF THE JOINT

These occur less frequently than the other joint defects that have been discussed. Cracking at the center of the joint is usually caused by stress built up from excess structural deflection or racking of the wall. Excess heat or moisture in the room can also be the cause.

To correct this defect, you must remove the cause of heat, moisture, or racking, and then retape the joint. Remove any tape that may have lost its bond to the panel. Sometimes control joints can be installed, allowing for some panel movement, especially if the crack was caused by moisture or excessively high temperatures. (See the use of control joints in Chapter 6.)

CORNER CRACKING

Sometimes the internal corners run a crack toward the ceiling. This can be prevented by placing very little joint compound at the actual intersection of the panels. Sometimes the tape is accidentally split with the finishing tool and the joint compound over this will surely crack. To correct, retape and refinish the joint. Consider using the floating interior-angle corner described in Chapter 6 (*page 62*) or a vinyl inside corner, as shown in Chapter 7.

STRESS CRACKS

It is not unusual for stresses that occur at the corners of doors, windows, and cased openings to cause a crack to run up the wall. This is generally caused by a settling of the wall or horizontal forces, causing very slight racking of the studs. The crack may be very slight and occur only along the front surface of the drywall. Greater stress can cause the crack to go completely through the panel.

Before starting a repair, press against the drywall to see if it has any movement. If it does, install additional nails or screws in the nearest studs on each side (**9–13**). Then, cut each side of the crack, forming a V-groove. Then fill the crack with drywall compound and lay fiberglass mesh tape over it. After it has hardened, finish with two or three coats of compound.

TAPE PHOTOGRAPHING

If the tape is still visible after several finish coats have been applied, it may have a slightly different color than the compound or have a gloss over it. This can be caused by taping in an area with high humidity (delays the drying of the compound) or by not pressing the tape firmly in place so the excess joint compound below it is forced out.

Photographing can also result if the wall is painted when the humidity is high or if poor-quality paint is used and coverage is inadequate. Some people seal the tape with a primer and apply additional coats of compound. Others prefer to add additional top coats, using a topping compound. Be certain to lower the humidity of the air.

JOINT DEPRESSIONS

If the center of the finished joint is lower than the sides, the depression formed will be very visible. Usually it occurs if the thickness of the finishing coats is too thin or if the compound mix is too thin. Correct this by making certain the finishing compound is the proper consistency and applying additional finish coats of a thickness needed to fill the depression.

CROWNING

Crowning refers to the development of an excessively high arcing of the joint compound over the joint. This produces a bulge or ridge that ruins the flat appearance of the wall.

To correct a crowning problem, sand down the bulge or ridge that has formed. Then recoat the area of the joint with joint compound. Feather it out wider than it was originally.

STARVED JOINTS

If a joint is recoated before the previous coat has had sufficient time to harden or if not enough joint compound was used in the first place, the joint may have a hollow concave surface due to shrinkage. Recoat the joint and allow sufficient drying time between coats. Use a low-shrinkage compound.

RIDGING

Ridging is a continuous ridge running the length of the joint-usually down the center. It is caused when panels are butted too tight, which places them under stress and causes the butting panels to bend out slightly along the joint.

To correct, let the wall react for several months and at least through a hot season. Then sand down the ridge and fill the concave areas with joint compound. Let it thoroughly dry before applying a final thin float coat over the entire area.

SEALING AROUND PIPES

Any open space between the drywall and pipes must be sealed, or it will be a major source of energy loss. If the pipes will not show, as under a sink, and the openings are not large, fill them with caulking. If they are too large for this, you can patch around them with tape (**9–14**).

While openings for things such as light fixtures and electrical outlet boxes can be cut accurately with a drywall router, occasionally the opening is a bit large or damaged on one side. This allows air to filter into the house, introducing contaminants and increasing heating and cooling bills. These perimeter openings can be sealed as shown in **9–15**. Here, fiberglass mesh tape is laid up over the opening. A special electrical outlet box seal is available and covers all four sides (**9–16**). It has an adhesive backing. After the mesh has been applied, several coats of joint compound are applied in the normal manner.

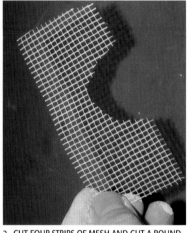

1. THIS PROTRUDING PIPE CAN BE SEALED WITH FIBERGLASS MESH TAPE.

2. CUT FOUR STRIPS OF MESH AND CUT A ROUND SECTION TO FIT NEXT TO THE PIPE.

3. APPLY JOINT COMPOUND TO THE WALLBOARD AND LAY IN ONE STRIP OF MESH.

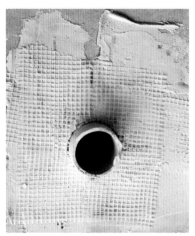

4. CONTINUE AROUND THE PIPE, LAYING MESH STRIPS ON ALL FOUR SIDES. THEN COVER WITH JOINT CEMENT.

▲ **9–14.** You can seal around pipes by cutting and fitting the tape to the pipes and finishing the area with joint compound in the normal manner.

Paint Problems

Often, after the finished panel is painted, various irregularities in the appearance of the surface are noticed. Following are the most common.

VARIATIONS IN PAINT APPEARANCE

Due to differences in the surface of the panel paper and the dried, sanded joint compound, the paint on these areas may vary from a sheen on the compound to a flat on the paper. This occurs over each joint and fastener. The difference is caused by the difference in suction in the two surfaces. When light hits the walls and ceilings, the difference can be quite pronounced.

To prevent this, seal the entire surface with a latex or solvent sealer or a coat of alkyd flat wall paint. Drywall

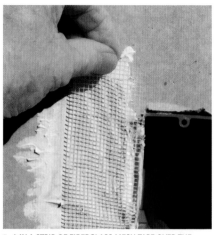

1. THE OPENING HAS BEEN CUT, LEAVING A LARGE GAP ON ONE SIDE.

2. FILL THE OPENING WITH JOINT COMPOUND.

3. LAY A STRIP OF FIBERGLASS MESH TAPE OVER THE AREA AND FINISH IN THE NORMAL MANNER.

▲ 9–15. When an opening, such as around an outlet box, has been cut too wide on one or more sides, fill the large opening with joint cement and lay a layer of fiberglass mesh over it. Finish in the normal manner.

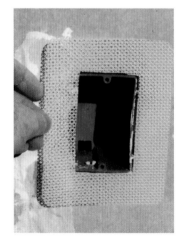

▲ 9–16. This special adhesive-backed patch is used to seal electrical outlet boxes.

manufacturers have a product designed especially to coat and seal the joint compound for painting. It provides a better base for paint than conventional sealers. These are applied by roller, brush, or spray.

VARIATIONS WHEN USING HIGH-GLOSS PAINTS

Again, the difference in suction in the gypsum panel paper and the joint compound produces a higher gloss on the areas covered with compound. To prevent this, apply a skim coat of joint compound over the entire surface.

DARKENING OF THE JOINTS

Sometimes the joints may tend to darken over time. This is usually caused when the paint is applied over a joint compound that has not been permitted to dry completely.

To reduce this occurrence, prime the joints with a latex- or solvent-based sealer or a white alkyd flat wall paint. Drywall manufacturers have a product designed especially to coat and seal the joint compound for painting. It provides a better base for paint than conventional sealers.

FINDING AND CORRECTING DEFECTS

Taping Joints and Finishing Trim and Corner Beads

10

AFTER THE DRYWALL PANELS *are installed and everything has been rechecked to be certain it is ready for finishing, the taping can begin. The panel with its paper cover is strong. Poorly taped joints tend to be the major place where a job may fail. It is very important that the joints be properly taped to resist cracking and to provide for the required fire protection expected from the finished wall.*

Before you begin taping, be certain that all fasteners are properly set, all openings—such as for electrical boxes—are properly cut, and the corner bead is installed properly. Make certain that the area in which you are working is ventilated and provision has been made to maintain the proper temperature (45 degrees F to 70 degrees F— approximately 7 degrees C to 21 degrees C).

Certain trestles or scaffolding needed for cathedral ceilings or other high surfaces are available (**10–1**). These must be quality units meeting federal OSHA safety requirements.

Make a Plan

Drywall finishers, through experience, develop a plan for the sequence of steps they follow. Various individuals and a full-time finisher will no doubt follow a different plan from the homeowners doing their own work. Some prefer to complete the ceiling before beginning the walls. Following is a six-step sequence that serves well for many people. It assumes the use of paper tape and three coats of joint compound.

1. Put the first coat over all fasteners and minor nicks on all walls of the room.
2. Put the first coat and tape on all horizontal and vertical joints.
3. Install corner tapes and when dry apply the second coat.
4. Put the first coat on trim and corner beads. When dry, apply the second coat.

5. Apply the second coat on the fasteners, horizontal, and vertical joints.
6. Apply the third coat on fasteners, joints, corners, and beads.

Some Things to Consider

1. Feather joints by running the knife on one side and then the other, and finish by stroking down the center.
2. When feathering, start at one end of the joint and do not lift the knife until you get to the other end.
3. After you have worked over the compound on a joint three or four times, it begins to get sticky and should not be worked any more.
4. Make certain the compound in your mud pan is stirred occasionally so that the consistency is constant.
5. If the compound has dry chunks of compound, discard it.

6. Keep the inside of your pan, the lid on the compound bucket, and the tools used to move it to the pan, free of dried lumps.
7. If there are ridges on the dried joint, remove them by scraping with a clean dry wall knife before applying the next coat.
8. Do not put compound on more joints than you know that you can finish before it starts to harden.
9. Before applying a coat of joint compound be certain the wall is free of sanding dust. Joint compound will not stick over sanding dust.

As you tape a job, you will be faced with tapered edge joints, square nontapered joints, inside and outside corner joints, as well as control joints. In addition, you will have to conceal fasteners and sometimes you will need to repair damage that has been done to the panel.

Covering Fasteners

Fastener heads are covered by passing a 5- or 6-inch taping knife loaded with joint compound over the head. Keep the blade almost flush with the panel (10–2). Then raise the knife to about a 45-degree angle and scrape off excess compound. You only want to fill the dimple. Some finishers will pass the trowel down a row of fasteners, covering several with one stroke (10–3). After this first coat is dry, repeat the operation until the dimple is flush with the surface.

Finishing Around Openings

Electrical outlets, light boxes, and other openings need to be finished so that when the installation is complete the compound flows smoothly behind the cover plate or light base. Hopefully the drywall opening was accurately located and cut to fit closely. In this case, fill the slight opening with compound and

▶ **10–1.** Scaffolding is one of the many items required for installing gypsum wallboard.

TAPING JOINTS AND FINISHING TRIM AND CORNER BEADS

lightly feather it away as shown in **10–4**. This provides the needed fire rating of the wall and seals the crack, reducing air infiltration. If the crack is so large that the compound falls out, you will have to place tape over the crack and finish as you would a joint.

Taping Tapered Joints

The first decision is whether to use paper of fiberglass mesh tape. Paper tape is stronger and can be used with a wide variety of joint compounds. Fiberglass mesh tape is easier to install but must be covered with a setting-type joint compound. The mesh tape is not strong enough to use on square butted end joints.

USING PAPER TAPE

The steps to finish a tapered joint are shown in **10–5**. Begin by laying down a coat of joint compound in the tapered area (**10–5A**). Use a 5- or 6-inch tapering knife and spread the compound in a rather even layer about ¼ inch thick. Do not work too far ahead of the actual taping or the compound may start to set. Now unroll a section of tape and press it lightly into the compound. The tape

should be long enough so that it covers the entire length of the joint. It should go all the way to the corner (**10–5B**).

Now, keeping the tape tight pull the taping knife along the tape, pressing it into the compound. The knife will be on a low angle (**10–5B**). This pushes out some of the joint compound from below the tape, leaving a layer about ⅛ inch thick in the cement and ¹⁄₃₂ inch on the edges to bond the tape to the wallboard. As you do this, excess compound will squeeze out at the edges and have to be removed. The finished first coat will have

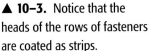

▲ **10–3.** Notice that the heads of the rows of fasteners are coated as strips.

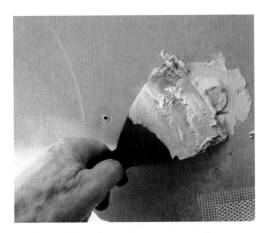

▲ **10–2.** The heads of fasteners are given a first coat of compound with a 4-inch taping knife. (*Courtesy National Gypsum Company*)

▲ **10–4.** The edges of this outlet box have been sealed to prevent leakage.

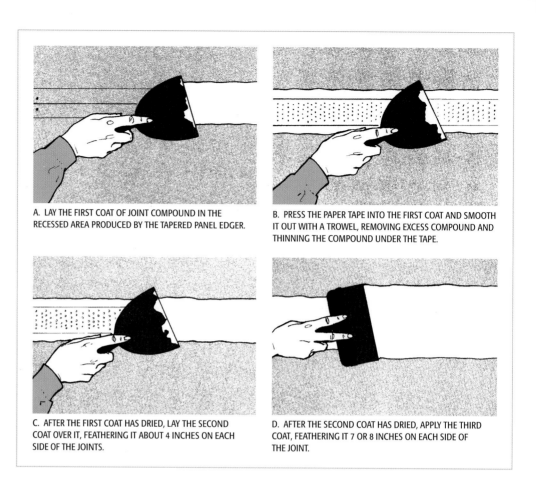

A. LAY THE FIRST COAT OF JOINT COMPOUND IN THE RECESSED AREA PRODUCED BY THE TAPERED PANEL EDGER.

B. PRESS THE PAPER TAPE INTO THE FIRST COAT AND SMOOTH IT OUT WITH A TROWEL, REMOVING EXCESS COMPOUND AND THINNING THE COMPOUND UNDER THE TAPE.

C. AFTER THE FIRST COAT HAS DRIED, LAY THE SECOND COAT OVER IT, FEATHERING IT ABOUT 4 INCHES ON EACH SIDE OF THE JOINTS.

D. AFTER THE SECOND COAT HAS DRIED, APPLY THE THIRD COAT, FEATHERING IT 7 OR 8 INCHES ON EACH SIDE OF THE JOINT.

the tape embedded and the compound feathered out on each side.

If the paper tape wrinkles, it means you may have not kept it pulled tight as you pressed it in the compound or you put down too thick a layer. You may have to remove it and reapply.

Sometimes you will cover a very long joint with two pieces of tape. Be certain they overlap at the center and work each from the center toward the corner.

Second Coat

The second coat (**10–5C**) adds additional compound to the tapered joint and helps fill the recess. Before you apply it, check the joint for smoothness. Remove any lumps or ridges. Usually the sharp edge of the taping knife will cut these off, leaving a relatively smooth surface. The second coat is applied after the first coat has dried. The drying will vary with the relative humidity, temperature, and the time lapsed. This can range for all-purpose compounds from around 10 hours for zero-percent relative humidity and 70° F (21° C) to 3 days (72 hrs.) if the relative humidity is 90 percent at 70° F. The second coat widens out the feathered area and is smoothed to blend into the panel as much as possible. It can be an all-purpose joint compound or a taping compound.

Apply the compound with a 6-inch taping knife and work the coating down with a 12- or 14-inch beveled trowel or finishing knife (**10–6**).

TAPING JOINTS AND FINISHING TRIM AND CORNER BEADS

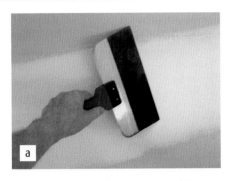

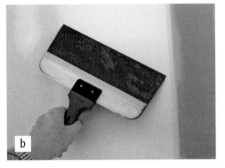

▲ **10–6.** The final finishing of the second coat of joint compound is best done with a 12- to 14-inch finishing knife.

Third (Finish) Coat

The third coat (**10–5D**) is usually just a very light skim coat. If you have done a good job of smoothly applying the first two coats, you will only need to do a little light sanding to prepare for this final coat. Usually a 100-grit or 120-grip sandpaper is used. Be certain to remove all gypsum dust from any sanding before applying the third coat. Feather the edges of the third coat about 2 inches wider so they flow into the paper on the panel (**10–7**). You can feel them with your hand or turn a light on them to see if there is any small edge left. Do not sand the paper surface because this will roughen it. If you do damage the paper, it will be necessary to float a very thin coat of joint compound over it.

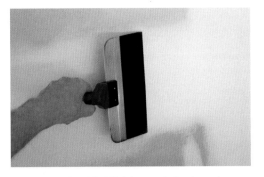

▲ **10–7.** The third finish coat is feathered several inches beyond the second coat with a finishing knife.

This third coat will be just a little wider than the second coat and is usually thinner. Remember to coat the fasteners with the same materials. The layers of a finished joint are shown in **10–8**.

Taping Abutted End Joints

The butted ends of panels have no tapered area to receive the joint compound as do the long edges of the panels, so require a wider feathered area to reduce notice of the large crown formed.

Before you secure butted ends to the framing, bevel them slightly on a 45-degree angle. This cuts away only raw paper edge. Be certain the ends are close but not touching (**10–9**).

Begin by applying the compound over the surface of the joint and embed the tape as described for tapered joints. Press the tape tightly against the panel, yet leave enough compound to bond it to the panel. After it dries, apply the second and third coats as described for a taper joint. To reduce the appearance of a crown, feather each layer about twice as wide as a taper edge joint. One such application is shown in **10–10**. Typically, the tape and compound on a finished abutted end joint will be $1/8$ to $1/16$ inch thick and 18 to 24 inches wide.

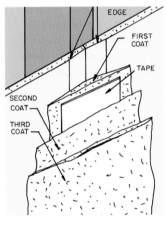

▲ **10–8.** A typical finished joint.

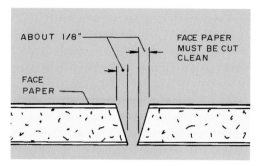

◄ 10-9. Cut a slight taper on the end of square-edge abutted panels. This removes any ragged paper edges and produces a clean, ridge-free gypsum core.

▼ 10-10. Any tool with a long, straight edge can be used to check for excess crowning.

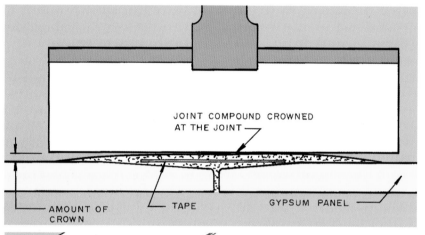

◄ 10-11. The paper tape has a crease in the center that helps you fold it for use on inside corners.

▼ 10-12. Steps for applying paper tape on an inside corner.

You can check the joint with a straightedge to see just how much of a crown exists (**10-10**). If it is excessive, apply additional coats of compound and widen the feathered area.

Taping the Corners

There are a number of types of inside and outside corner beads available. The types and installation are covered in detail in Chapter 7.

TAPING INSIDE CORNERS

Inside corners should be taped with paper tape or plastic tape inside corner beads (see Chapter 7). Fiberglass mesh will not fold to form a permanent corner. The trick to an inside corner is to get both sides covered with compound without messing up one of the sides of the tape.

Begin by laying joint compound on both sides of the inside corner. Usually, a 4-inch layer around ⅛ inch thick will be used. Fold the paper tape along the crease in the center (**10-11**). Starting at the ceiling, press the tape into the compound. Keep the tape tight as you move down the wall. Remove any wrinkles (**10-12**).

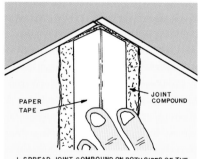

1. SPREAD JOINT COMPOUND ON BOTH SIDES OF THE CORNER AND PRESS THE TAPE INTO THE COMPOUND. WORK OUT ANY WRINKLES.

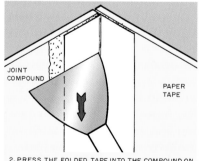

2. PRESS THE FOLDED TAPE INTO THE COMPOUND ON ONE SIDE. BE CAREFUL YOU DO NOT PUNCTURE THE TAPE IN THE CORNER.

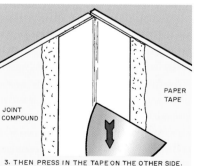

3. THEN PRESS IN THE TAPE ON THE OTHER SIDE. AGAIN, DO NOT DISTURB THE COMPOUND ON THE OTHER SIDE.

TAPING JOINTS AND FINISHING TRIM AND CORNER BEADS

▲ **10–13.** This rubber wipe-down knife is used to tape and wipe down the compound on an inside corner. It gets both sides in a single pass and will not damage paper tape. *(Courtesy Kraft Tool Company)*

The tape can be pressed into the compound on the wallboard with the flexible rubber-blade wipe-down knife shown in **10–13.** After the compound has hardened, the second and third coats are applied as discussed earlier. Work carefully so you do not cut through the tape or disturb the compound below the tape. A 6-inch taping knife is wide enough for this job (**10–14**). Feather each layer a little beyond the layer below. A stainless-steel inside corner tool with a flexible blade can be used to do both sides of the corner with a single pass (**10–15**). There is also a rubber blade corner trowel that will dress both sides of the corner (**10–16**).

Often a gap will occur between the wall panels and ceiling panels. If the gap is less than ¼ inch, fill it with joint compound. When the compound is dry, apply the tape in the usual manner (**10–17**). Large gaps must be covered with adhesive-backed fiberglass tape. Press it firmly to the wall and ceiling. Then finish with joint compound in the normal manner (**10–18**).

▲ **10–16.** This flexible rubber-blade wipe-down knife will smooth the finish compound on both sides of a corner joint.

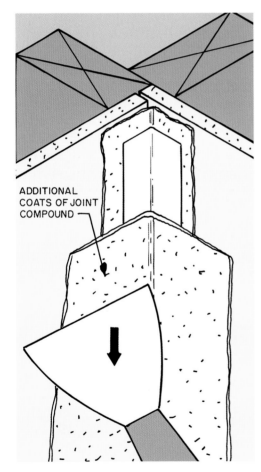

ADDITIONAL COATS OF JOINT COMPOUND

▲ **10–14.** After the tape has been embedded in the joint compound and it has hardened, apply several finish coats of compound over the tape. Each layer is feathered out a little beyond the previous coat.

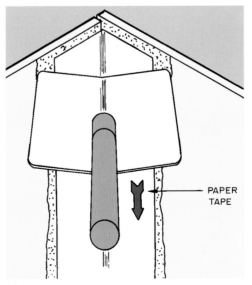

PAPER TAPE

▲ **10–15.** This corner trowel can be used to smooth the joint compound on both sides of the inside corner with a single pass.

▲ **10–17.** Very small gaps at the ceiling can be filled with joint compound.

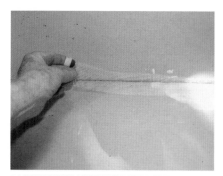

1. LAY ADHESIVE-BACKED MESH TAPE OVER THE CRACK. SOMETIMES A SECOND LAYER IS NEEDED ON WIDER CRACKS.

2. APPLY A LAYER OF JOINT COMPOUND OVER THE MESH TAPE.

3. LAY PRE-CREASED PAPER TAPE OVER THE CORNER AND FINISH IN THE NORMAL MANNER.

▲ **10–18.** Larger gaps at the ceiling should be covered with adhesive-backed fiberglass tape and finished with paper tape and joint compound.

▲ **10–19.** Clean, sharp corners are an indication of a quality job.

Finishing Exterior Corners

Exterior corners are subject to damage from day to day, so are finished by installing plastic or metal corner beads (**10–19**). Various types of beads are shown in Chapter 7. They can be installed with nails or staples. Each corner bead should run unbroken the full length of the corner.

After the beads are in place, run joint compound over the flanges, forcing it into the openings and feathering it out of the wall (**10–20**). A 6-inch taping knife is a good size to use. Hold the knife on a 45-degree angle and smooth the compound by letting one side of the blade slide along the center of the corner bead and the other over the surface of the panel. Use enough compound to get it to flow about 4 inches out on the panel. After it dries, additional coats can be applied until the coating extends about 6 to 8 inches from the corner (**10–21**). A typical detail is shown in **10–22**.

A typical bullnose corner bead installation is in **10–23**. It is installed and finished as just described. Another finishing bead is used to cover the exposed raw ends of the panels. The trim is placed over the end of the panel, and the panel

▲ **10–20.** Run the joint compound over the bead, pressing it firmly so it bonds to the wallboard through the perforations in the bead.

TAPING JOINTS AND FINISHING TRIM AND CORNER BEADS

▲ 10–21. Apply additional coats over the corner bead, feathering the compound out on the wall.

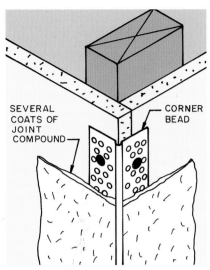

▲ 10–22. A typical finished exterior corner.

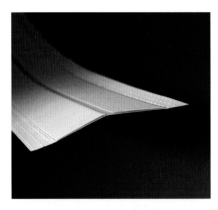

▲ 10–23. This special corner bead has a tapered plastic membrane over which a special finish paper is laid. *(Courtesy Structus Building Technologies, Inc.)*

is nailed to the framing. The exposed flange is finished with several coats of joint compound in the normal manner.

The No-Coat Corner System

This system uses a corner bead that has a tapered plastic membrane surfaced with a special paper cover (**10–23**). The corner is bonded to the drywall. The paper flap is also bonded with a small amount of all-purpose joint compound. It fits snugly and eliminates the need to finish the corner with additional coats of joint cement (**10–24**). See Chapter 7 for installation details.

Finishing Control Joints

Control joints have flanges that are fastened to the sides of panels spaced ½ inch apart. Apply joint compound to the flanges and feather it out about 4 inches; then apply two more coats as described for other trim and beads. These two coats will completely cover the joint because the opening of the V-shape is covered with a tape. After the final coat of compound, remove the plastic tape that reveals the inside of the control joint (**10–25**).

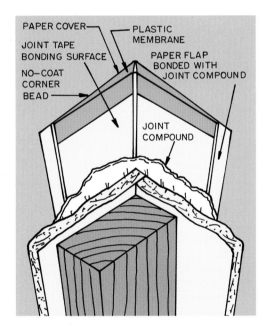

◀ 10–24. This tapered plastic corner bead and its paper flaps are bonded to the drywall. *(Courtesy Structus Building Technologies, Inc.)*

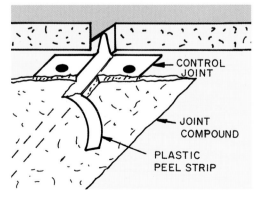

◀ 10–25. The control flanges are treated the same as various corner beads. The peel strip is pulled after the compound has set up. This allows the joint to expand as needed.

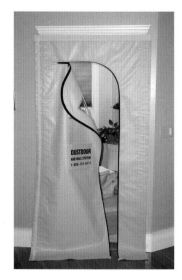

▲ **10–26**. Dust doors effectively seal off openings between rooms so dust from sanding is confined to one area. *(Courtesy Brophy Design, Inc.)*

▲ **10–27**. An experienced finisher can use stilts and a power sander to speed up the finishing of high areas.

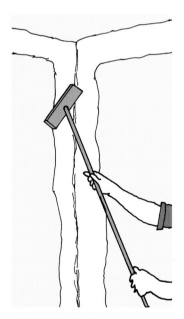

▲ **10–28**. A pole sander permits you to sand high areas on the walls and the ceiling while standing on the floor.

Sanding

Sanding produces a lot of very fine gypsum particles. They flow everywhere and are hazardous to your health. You must wear a dust mask that really filters the particles. The typical low-cost discardable mask must be replaced frequently and is considered by many as inadequate. What you need is a mask that has a heavy replaceable filter pad that does not let the particles in around the edges (see Chapter 8). In some places, a hard hat is required. It does provide protection for your head, but is often bulky. You do need some type of hat to keep your hair protected from dust.

Sanding the ceiling causes more difficulty from dust than sanding the walls.

Several manufacturers have pole-type dusters connected to a wet/dry-type vacuum that greatly reduces the dust in the air (see Chapter 8).

In new construction, it does not matter a great deal if the dust filters into adjoining rooms. A room addition or remodeling presents a case where you need to keep the dust within the room. You can do this by sealing the doors or arched openings with sheet plastic. The edges should be tightly taped to the wall or trim. Several manufacturers make "dust doors," designed for quick installation and providing a good seal. Some can be opened to allow a worker to pass through (**10–26**).

SANDING STEPS

Some finishers use power sanders, but they cut fast, can damage the paper, and are difficult for inexperienced people to use (**10–27**). They will probably cause more damage than good if you are inexperienced. If used, work very carefully. It only takes a few seconds to cut through to the tape. Then it is necessary to re-coat the surface with a joint compound.

More typically you will begin by using a pole sander rather than a power sander to remove any excess buildup on the fasteners and joints. Be attentive and very careful as you proceed. Crowned surfaces are especially a problem. Then finish with some type of hand sander.

POLE SANDING

The pole sander is used for the first sanding and, if used properly, will leave very little finish sanding to be done (**10–28**). The grit of the sanding screen to be used varies with how good a taping job you did. Either a 100- or 120-grit

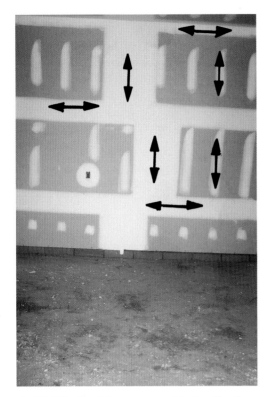

▲ **10–29.** Sand the compound in the direction of the joint or row of fasteners.

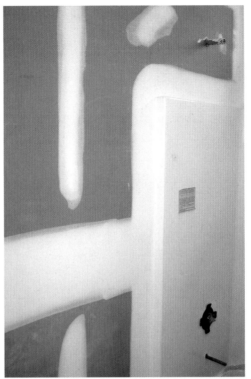

▲ **10–30.** The moisture-resistant wallboard abutting the edge of the fiberglass shower has been carefully taped, finished, and sanded.

screen is good. You may want to finish up with a 150-grit screen.

Sand the compound over the fasteners in the direction in which you applied the compound (**10–29**). Keep a good lookout for fasteners that were not properly secured. You may find that you have to make repairs and then re-coat some areas. Apply enough pressure on the pad to make it cut, but do not press too hard. Gentle is the touch.

If there is a large chunk of compound, cut it off with a finishing knife. Most small ridges can be sanded down. Inside corners require special care because the compound layer is rather thin. In general, work the area near the inside edge of the corner with a hand sander or a folded piece of sanding paper.

If you see defects—such as a long, deep scratch caused by a lump of compound—re-coat the area rather than trying to sand it out. Any seams that are underfilled need to be recoated. Excessive crowns may need to be re-coated and feathered wider. Then re-sand when dry. The sanding process reveals these defects. They should be corrected as soon as you notice them so that they can dry and be resanded as soon as possible.

When you are sanding around things already installed, such as bathtubs and showers, be especially careful you do not scratch their surface. Some units, e.g., a fiberglass shower (**10–30**), can be easily damaged. You may want to carefully hand-sand these with a folded piece of sanding paper.

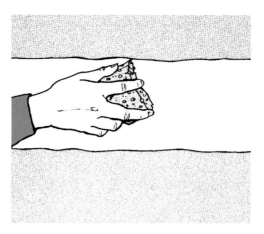

▶ **10–31.** Hand-sanding is done in the direction of the joint or row of fasteners. It is a very light sanding, producing the final finished surface.

HAND SANDING

After the pole sanding is finished, hopefully all defects have been corrected. This is the final touch-up of the surface and requires close inspection. Good lighting helps reveal areas needing special care. A portable light on a stand is very helpful.

Usually the hand sanding is done with 150-grit or finer sanding paper. Carefully, gently sand over all fasteners, joints, and corners. Visually keep a lookout for defects (**10–31**). Run your hand over the surface to try to feel for areas needing additional sanding. Areas in which the hand sander will not fit easily can be sanded with folded pieces of sanding paper. Sand in the direction of the joint or the row of fasteners.

WET SANDING

An alternate sanding method is wet sanding. It involves blending in the edges of the joint compound by stroking them with a wet sponge. This technique requires a certain level of experience. Aside from this mention, wet sanding will not be covered in this book.

When You Are Finished

Cleanup can be a big job. After taping, the lumps of compound that fall on the floor should be scraped up and removed. The gypsum dust is best removed with a commercial wet/dry vacuum. Remember, the dust filters everywhere-around windows, under doors, into electrical boxes. A thorough cleanup is necessary so that painting or wallpapering can begin.

Texturing and
Decorating Drywall

11

TEXTURED GYPSUM SURFACES *provide a wide variety of decorative treatments and also can help to cover any minor imperfections that might still be present in the wall-board surface. It is recommended that textured surface not be used in areas with high humidity.*

Also, remember that texture compound adds weight to the drywall. Since the compound is wet and heavy, it could cause a ceiling to sag. To avoid this, always use ½-inch drywall on the ceiling with joists spaced not over 16 inches O.C. If ⅝-inch drywall is used, the joists can be spaced 24 inches.

Another possibility is using high-strength gypsum ceiling panels. They resist sagging and warping. Check the manufacturer's installation instructions to verify the thickness recommended. Texture application requires the air and drywall to be at least 55° F (13° C) and kept above that temperature as it cures. The room should also have some ventilation.

Texture Finishing Materials

Texturing can be done with standard joint compound, all-purpose joint compound, topping compound, or a premixed texturing compound.

Textures may be applied by hand or with special spray equipment. Manufacturers have available a wide range of texture materials for both hand and spray application. Some are in powder form and are mixed with water, while others are premixed. The aggregate materials in the mix, such as silica sand, produce textures from very fine to heavy and coarse. Some materials can have a tint added, whereas others can be nearly

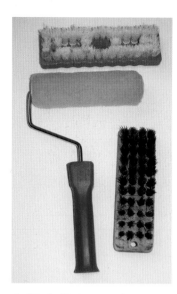

▲ **11–1.** Texture can be produced by using many objects commonly available in the home.

white. Such whitish materials must be painted if a colored surface is desired.

You can add small amounts of water to the texturing compound if you want a thinner application. Likewise, small amounts of aggregate can also be added if you would like to change the texture. If you choose to do either of these alterations in the mixture, measure the amounts added carefully so that each batch has the same fluidity and texture.

Hand-Texturing Tools

The hand tools used to create textured patterns are many and varied. Most often they are some type of brush, sponge, roller, or trowel. You will find many of these in your home (**11–1**).

The common available hand-texturing tools used by drywall finishers are shown in **11–2**.

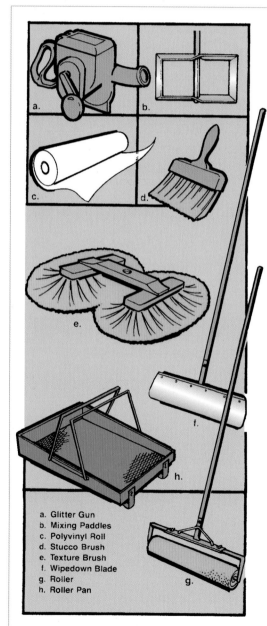

a. Glitter Gun
b. Mixing Paddles
c. Polyvinyl Roll
d. Stucco Brush
e. Texture Brush
f. Wipedown Blade
g. Roller
h. Roller Pan

A. THE GLITTER GUN IS FOR EMBEDDING GLITTER IN WET TEXTURED CEILINGS. THE HAND-CRANK MODEL SHOWN IS MOST ECONOMICAL BUT IT IS NOT AS EFFICIENT AS THE AIR-POWERED TYPE (NOT SHOWN).

B. MIXING PADDLES ARE AVAILABLE IN VARIOUS STYLES. PADDLES ARE USED WITH A HEAVY-DUTY ½-INCH ELECTRIC DRILL FOR THOROUGH, TIME-SAVING MIXING OF JOINT COMPOUNDS AND TEXTURING PRODUCTS.

C. POLYVINYL ROLL MATERIAL IS USED TO PROTECT DOORS, WINDOWS, AND OTHER THINGS IN THE ROOM.

D. THE STUCCO BRUSH IS USED FOR CREATING A VARIETY OF TEXTURES FROM STIPPLE TO SWIRL. OTHER VARIATIONS CAN BE ACHIEVED WITH THICKER APPLICATION AND DEEPER TEXTURING.

E. TEXTURE BRUSHES ARE AVAILABLE IN MANY SIZES AND STYLES; TANDEM-MOUNTED BRUSHES COVER A LARGE AREA TO SPEED THE JOB.

F. A WIPE-DOWN BLADE HAS A HARDENED STEEL BLADE AND A LONG HANDLE TO SPEED THE CLEANING OF WALLS AND FLOORS AFTER THE APPLICATION OF JOINT COMPOUND OR TEXTURE MATERIALS. THE BLADE HAS ROUNDED CORNERS TO PREVENT GOUGING.

G. THE STANDARD PAINT ROLLER IS ADAPTED TO THE PARTICULAR TYPE OF FINISH REQUIRED. SEVERAL VARIETIES OF ROLLER SLEEVE ARE AVAILABLE INCLUDING SHORT-NAP, LONG-NAP, AND CARPET TYPES IN PROFESSIONAL WIDTHS.

H. THE ROLLER PAN IS FOR USE WITH THE ROLLERS. SOME MODELS CAN HOLD UP TO A 25-POUND SUPPLY OF MIXED TEXTURE MATERIAL.

▶ **11–2.** Equipment used for hand-texturing walls and ceilings. *(Courtesy United States Gypsum Corporation)*

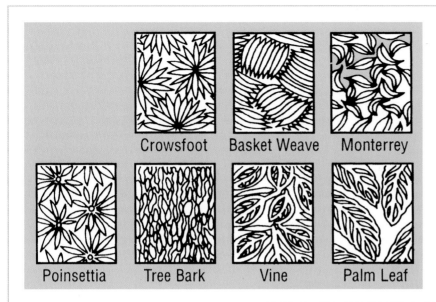

Crowfoot Basket Weave Monterrey

Poinsettia Tree Bark Vine Palm Leaf

Rollers and various pads with long handles are available; they let you texture the ceiling as you stand on the floor. When you use small brushes and sponges you will need a ladder or scaffolding. There are also available a series of rollers with textured surfaces that can enable you to roll on a uniform, repetitive texture. They fit on a standard 9-inch paint roller (**11–3**).

SPRAY-TEXTURING EQUIPMENT

A spray-texturing machine is shown in **11–4**. The texture compound is fed to a spray nozzle from a hopper. Compressed air is introduced at the nozzle-where the compound is atomized and sprayed on the wall or ceiling.

Preparation for Texturing

Before doing anything, finish the joints and cover the heads of fasteners the same as you would if you were going to paint the wall. Do a good job. Texture will hide small defects, but most defects will show even when textured. Some finishers only apply two coats of compound. This is satisfactory if a good job is done and the material is feathered out sufficiently.

▲ **11–3.** These special rollers can produce a variety of textures when rolled over a freshly textured surface. *(Courtesy Kraft Tool Company)*

◄ **11–4.** A spray-texturing machine with compound hopper. The hopper holds the texture compound that is sprayed by compressed air through a nozzle at the bottom of the hopper. *(Courtesy Kraft Tool Company)*

Now you should cover the surface with a primer coating (available from the dry-wall manufacturer) or at least a coat of alkyd paint or a latex-based primer. When you do this, you will have sealed the surface at the joints so it has the same degree of absorption as the paper. This greatly reduces the chance that fasteners and taped joints will show through.

Manual Application of the Texture Compound

Texture compound is manually applied with a trowel or roller.

ROLLER TEXTURE APPLICATION

The easiest way to apply the compound is with a roller on a long handle. Put the compound in a roller pan. It will hold about 25 pounds of compound. Roll the roller in the compound, being careful not to load it up too much. Apply

▶ 11–5. When rolling on texture compound, be sure to follow a predetermined plan.

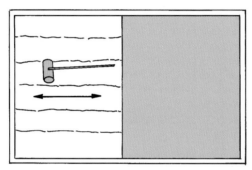

1. ROLL THE TEXTURE COMPOUND OVER PART OF THE CEILING PARALLEL WITH ONE WALL.

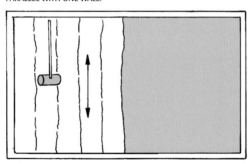

2. ROLL A SECOND LAYER OF TEXTURE COMPOUND OVER THE FIRST LAYER AND PERPENDICULAR TO IT.

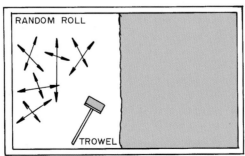

3. MOVE THE ROLLER IN RANDOM DIRECTIONS TO SMOOTH AND PRODUCE THE DESIRED FINISH, OR LIGHTLY TROWEL THE SURFACE.

compound to the ceiling much like you paint with rollers.

It is necessary that you establish a regular plan for applying the texture compound. This will produce uniform results in every room you finish.

One plan is to begin in a corner along a wall. Be very careful to keep the compound off the wall. To do this you can tape (masking tape) a piece of paper or plastic on the wall so that it touches the ceiling. Generally the large ceiling area will be textured by breaking it up into smaller areas such as 6 × 6 feet or 8 × 8 feet. If you work rapidly, much larger areas can be covered and, perhaps, all of a small room. Roll the first layer parallel with one wall. Keep the coating thin. Then roll a second coat over the first coat perpendicular to the first coat (**11–5**). After the second coat you may want to roll over the surface with the roller (do not add more compound) just to smooth and touch it up. This is done by rolling at random angles as you see a need for touching up the finish. Now repeat this for another area. Let it overlap slightly with the first area, and clear this up with the final smoothing roll.

If the compound begins to dry and you wish to touch up an area, do it with the roller. Coat it with a very thin coating. A brush will damage the texture, leaving a visible defect. Usually you will have to thin the prepared texture compound so it will flow off the roller. If you get it too thin, it is going to run down the roller handle and across your arms as well as drop off the ceiling.

If you prefer, you can lightly trowel the applied rolled texture compound to get a slightly different look.

Hand-Texturing Examples

The texture patterns are limited only by your imagination. Following are some of the conventional types.

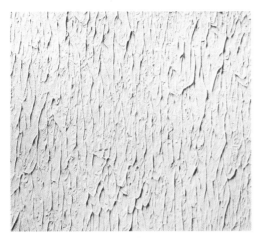

▲ **11–6.** This texture was produced with a long-napped roller. *(Courtesy United States Gypsum Corporation)*

▲ **11–7.** A stippled texture created with a round texture brush. *(Courtesy United States Gypsum Corporation)*

▲ **11–8.** These texture brushes will create a stippled surface. The pattern will vary because the smaller brushes have stiffer bristles. *(Courtesy Kraft Tool Company)*

ROLLER PATTERNS

Illustration 11–6 shows a texture produced by a long-napped paint roller. The degree of coarseness is produced by the texture of the roller sleeve. Try it out on some scrap before doing the ceiling. The fabric sleeve can be removed and other types bought and installed.

STIPPLED PATTERNS

A very fine stippled finish (**11–7**) can be produced by a texture brush like those shown in **11–8**. Brushes with coarser bristles will produce a slightly different texture. Remember, first experiment on some scrap stock.

To stipple a surface with joint compound, use a mud pan and a brush of your choice. While any brush will do, special brushes are available. Place the brush in the compound and then press to the surface. Each impression should touch or blend with the one beside it. Most prefer to work on an area such as 6 × 6 or 8 × 8 feet. Finish it and move on down the ceiling. Usually you will want to go over the area lightly with a finishing knife to even it up. Do this before the compound begins to harden.

SPONGE PATTERNS

By placing a rather open-surfaced sponge in joint compound and pressing it to the surface, you will get a texture resembling that in **11–9**. The shape of the image can be regulated by cutting the sponge to some shape, such as a circle or ellipse. As you press it to the surface, overlap each impression and vary the sponge's angle.

◄ **11–9.** This is typical of textures that can be made by pressing a sponge coated with compound against the drywall.

▶ **11–10.** Swirl patterns can be produced by rotating a brush in the layer of joint compound that's rolled on the surface.

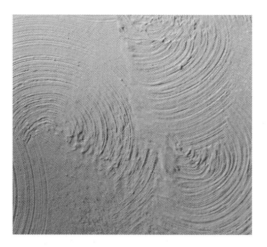

SWIRL PATTERNS

Begin by rolling on a layer of joint compound. Then place your brush on this surface and twist to produce a texture like the one shown in **11–10**. The swirls can be made at random angles to each other or be lined up in carefully placed rows.

TROWELED PATTERNS

Troweled textures are heavier and more pronounced than those made with a brush or sponge. In **11–11** a texture is shown that has been laid down with a hand trowel. The size of the blade will influence the overall pattern. This is a heavy texture.

▶ **11–11.** After the texture compound has been applied to the surface, it can be smoothed and the texture varied with a trowel. *(Courtesy United States Gypsum Corporation)*

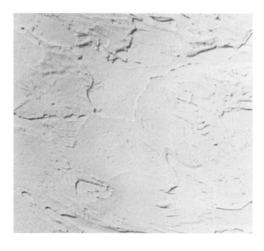

To apply a troweled texture, you will need a trowel or taping knife. A 10- or 12-inch taping knife is frequently used. The larger tools will cover more area faster but require more strength to move across the surface.

1. Begin by placing the texture compound on the blade of the trowel. It should extend across the width of the blade.
2. Place the edge of the blade about $\frac{1}{2}$ to 1 inch above the surface of the panel. Make a sweep across the surface, laying out about a $\frac{1}{16}$- to $\frac{1}{8}$-inch thick layer.
3. Now go back over the area with the trowel and even the compound. You can vary the angle of the trowel to produce the look you want. Do not overtrowel, because doing so will cause a tearing of the compound.
4. Repeat this on an area next to the first effort and blend them together. Continue with area after area until the ceiling is covered. This produces a fairly smooth thin coat of texture compound.

You can produce a more dramatic appearance by using a procedure often referred to as "skip-texture." The surface produced is much rougher than that produced with the ordinary trowel method. However, the degree of roughness can be regulated by the movement and pressure placed on the trowel.

To apply a skip-texture, use a large trowel:

1. Put a heavy coating of texture compound on the trowel. It should cover the entire length of the blade.
2. Place the edge of the blade just above the surface of the drywall panel and then move the blade across the surface. This action will deposit a layer of compound on the surface.

3. As you draw the blade across the surface, lower the angle. With experience you will find out how much pressure to use. In general a light pressure is best. This will apply the compound in irregularly shaped deposits—some parts of the drywall getting no coating. This is the result you should try to achieve.

4. Now draw the trowel back across these deposits—carefully smoothing them and getting a fairly consistent height (**11–12**). This will leave some flattened high spots and some areas with no compound-producing the particular rough texture you desire.

5. Continue across the ceiling, working each trowel load of compound as you go. Carefully work the areas as they abut each other so that you are able to achieve a smooth transition.

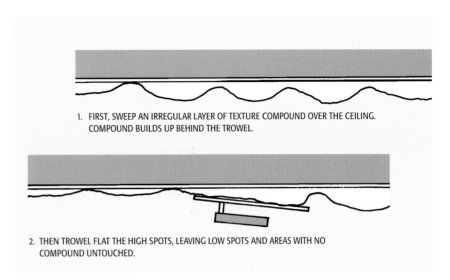

1. FIRST, SWEEP AN IRREGULAR LAYER OF TEXTURE COMPOUND OVER THE CEILING. COMPOUND BUILDS UP BEHIND THE TROWEL.

2. THEN TROWEL FLAT THE HIGH SPOTS, LEAVING LOW SPOTS AND AREAS WITH NO COMPOUND UNTOUCHED.

▲ **11–12.** After the texture compound has been applied roughly to the surface, a trowel is run over it, leveling some of the high places and leaving low places untouched.

Glitter

Glitter is a shiny material that comes in the form of fine granules. After the texture compound has been applied, glitter is sprayed on it with a glitter gun (**11–13**). While you can manually broadcast it toward the surface, this tends to gives a very uneven coating. The glitter gun sprays the material in an even pattern-much like the device used to spray grass seed and granular fertilizer over a lawn. The application of the glitter must be done before the texturing compound hardens. Glitter can also be applied to a wet painted surface.

◀ **11–13.** A glitter gun is used to apply glitter to ceilings and walls. (*Courtesy Kraft Tool Company*)

Spray Textures

Several of the many spray texture finishes are in **11–14**. Spray-texturing requires spray equipment and some experience. Since it tends to overspray, your doors, windows and trim (if installed) should be covered. Drywall finishers use a spray shield (**11–15**) to keep overspray off walls, window frames, and floors. It is placed over the surface to be protected as the drywall in that area is textured. You can also use masking tape and plastic sheets, but this is time-consuming. If

► **11–14.** Some of the texture patterns available for use with spray equipment. *(Courtesy National Gypsum Company)*

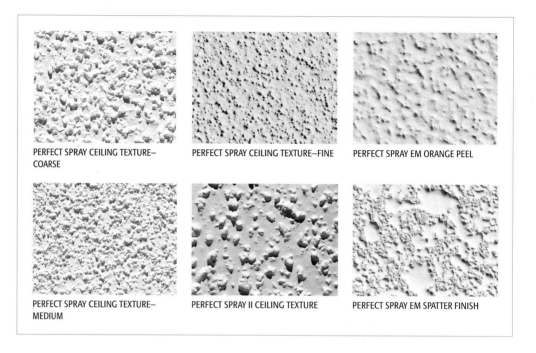

PERFECT SPRAY CEILING TEXTURE–COARSE

PERFECT SPRAY CEILING TEXTURE–FINE

PERFECT SPRAY EM ORANGE PEEL

PERFECT SPRAY CEILING TEXTURE–MEDIUM

PERFECT SPRAY II CEILING TEXTURE

PERFECT SPRAY EM SPATTER FINISH

▲ **11–15.** A spray shield is used to protect surfaces from overspray while texturing. *(Courtesy Kraft Tool Company)*

► **11–16.** The hand-held hopper on the spray equipment applies the texture compound to the ceiling.

HOPPER HOLDS COMPOUND

MASK & GOGGLES

NOZZLE SPRAYS COMPOUND

COMPRESSED AIR HOSE

some gets on the wall use a finishing knife to scrape it off. After the surface has hardened, a light sanding will smooth it up.

An acoustic spray-applied texture gives a sound-absorbing, sound-rated decorative finish to gypsum panels, concrete, and some types of plaster ceilings. This treatment can help meet code regulations for sound transmission control.

The spray equipment consists of an air compressor, a hand-held hopper (refer to **11–4**) containing the texture compound, and a hose with a nozzle, from which the compound is atomized and applied to the gypsum wallboard (**11–16**).

Texture Paints

Texture paints are a heavy latex interior paint that has a texturing additive. It is a little thinner than joint compound. However, it is thicker than regular latex paint. When applied to the surface with a roller or sponge it gives a light, stippled finish. Read the manufacturer's instructions before proceeding with the application.

Preparation for Painting

After the drywall has been taped and sanded, it is generally painted. However, it can be textured or covered with wallpaper, vinyl wall covering, fabric, or some other material.

PREPARING THE SURFACE FOR PAINTING

Assuming that the taping and sanding was satisfactorily completed and all minor defects have been repaired, the wall is ready to paint. It should be clean and have no materials, such as adhesives or oil, that will keep the paint from bonding. Use a vacuum or at least clean rags or brushes to remove sanding dust.

APPLY THE PRIME OR SEALER COAT

The first coat is the **prime coat**. It should be the one recommended by the manufacturer of the finish paint you plan to use. It will have fillers and pigments that equalize the absorption properties of the finished wall, and it provides a base upon which the finish coat can bond.

Sometimes the taped joints and fasteners "photograph" (i.e., show) through even the final coat of paint. The primer or sealer will help reduce this.

The wall may be coated with a **sealer** instead of a primer. It contains a resin and is better suited for equalizing the porosity of the surface than most primers. Photographing can occur even with a sealer.

Also on the market is a primer-sealer. It provides good results and is often used.

One way to totally eliminate photographing is to skim-coat the drywall. This involves covering the entire wall with a thin coat of joint compound after the joints have had their three coats. This is time-consuming and expensive, so is not done except on the jobs requiring the highest quality. After skim-coating, the wall must be sanded and sealer-primer must still be applied.

Skim coating can be done with all-purpose joint compound or a special covering compound. Keep the consistency about the same as when taping joints. Apply with a wide trowel, joint knife, or long nap roller. The coating should be very thin. Then wipe down the surface with a broad finishing knife to get the final deposits as thin and smooth as possible.

Preparing Drywall for Wallcover Materials

It is a common practice to apply regular wallpaper, fabric-backed wallpaper, and paper-vinyl-backed fabric wallcovering materials over the finished drywall surface. The surface should be taped and finished as described earlier in this chapter. While some heavy fabric coverings will hide small surface blemishes, many regular papers will not.

Since these wallcoverings are applied wet, it is necessary to seal the wall surface so the moisture will not soften the joint compound. After three coats of joint compound are applied and sanded smooth, apply a coat of white flat latex wall paint. After this is dry, apply a primer-sizer coat to prepare the surface to accept the adhesive-backed wallcovering.

12 Other Useful Applications

GYPSUM PANELS ARE USED *for many applications besides finishing interior walls and ceilings. The following examples illustrate some that are useful for residential and light commercial construction.*

Steel Studs and Joists

Steel studs have been used extensively in commercial construction for many years. More recently, they are being used for residential exterior wall and interior partition framing.

The metal stud wall will be installed by others—as is the case with wood stud walls. The metal studs are cut to length so that they are a little shorter than the floor to ceiling length as shown in **12–1**. The wall is assembled by securing the metal track to the floor. Then, using a plumb line, the ceiling track is located and secured to the ceiling. The studs are usually joined to the tracks with sheet-metal screws (**12–2**).

Your job as finisher is to apply the gypsum wallboard to this metal framework. A typical metal stud partition and wall are shown in **12–3**.

Before hanging the drywall check the walls to be certain they are straight and plumb as discussed for wood-framed walls. Make certain the open sides on the studs all face the same direction (refer to **12–5**). Check the building inspection record on the job to be certain that the electrical work, plumbing, and other trades have completed their work and they have passed inspection before you start to work.

Gypsum drywall is installed on metal studs with self-drilling self-tapping steel

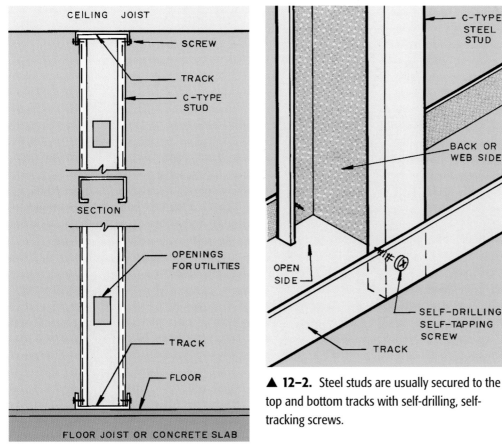

▲ **12–1.** A typical C-type steel stud installation.

▲ **12–2.** Steel studs are usually secured to the top and bottom tracks with self-drilling, self-tracking screws.

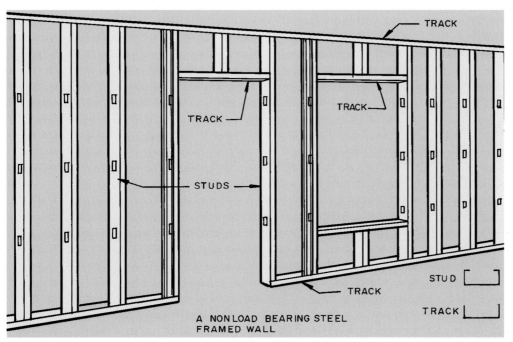

▶ **12–3.** This is a typical steel-framed, nonload-bearing wall that has been framed with C-type studs and tracks.

STEEL STUDS AND JOISTS

▲ 12–4. When driving screws, be certain to install them perpendicular to the face of the gypsum wallboard. *(Courtesy PAM Fastening Technology)*

▼ 12–5. Always join abutting panels by securing the panel on the open side of the stud first. After that panel is secure, install the abutting panel.

experience, you will know what setting to use. If you are not certain, drive a few screws into scrap pieces of stud. The screw head should be recessed slightly below the surface of the panel but not break the paper or the core. It is especially important to drive the screws straight. When the screw is set the correct depth, the screw gun head will automatically stop and the clutch releases the screw.

Single-layer gypsum wallboard can be applied horizontally or vertically as described for wood stud application. All edges and ends of the panels should be located in the center of the metal stud. Begin securing the panel by starting with the lead edge or end attached to the open side of the stud. Fasten the entire edge to this open edge and finish installing the panel. Then abut the next panel to it and set the screw close to the stud web (the solid side). Set all screws next to the web—except as described earlier for an end joint. If you join the solid side before the open side, the screw will tend to bend the open end out so that the panels will not abut squarely (**12–5**).

Screws in single-layer applications are spaced 16 inches O.C. when the steel studs are spaced 16 inches O.C. Ceilings are secured to steel joists with screws spaced 12 inches O.C. when the joists are spaced 16 inches O.C.

screws. The tips are designed to drill through the steel stud and the threads provide great holding power. Type-S bugle-head screws are used. (These are shown in Chapter 3.) Panels ½ inch thick require a 1-inch-long screw. They are driven with an electric screw gun (**12–4**). (Screw guns are described in Chapters 2 and 5.)

The screw gun can be adjusted to drive the screw to the proper depth. With

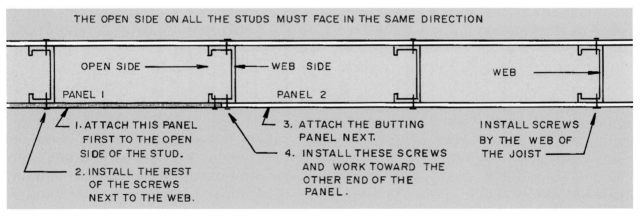

THE OPEN SIDE ON ALL THE STUDS MUST FACE IN THE SAME DIRECTION

OPEN SIDE ⟶   ⟵ WEB SIDE   WEB ⟶

PANEL 1   PANEL 2

1. ATTACH THIS PANEL FIRST TO THE OPEN SIDE OF THE STUD.

2. INSTALL THE REST OF THE SCREWS NEXT TO THE WEB.

3. ATTACH THE BUTTING PANEL NEXT.

4. INSTALL THESE SCREWS AND WORK TOWARD THE OTHER END OF THE PANEL.

INSTALL SCREWS BY THE WEB OF THE JOIST

Sound Isolation

Gypsum wallboard contributes a great deal to the reduction of sound through a wall, floor, or ceiling. If it is combined with various other materials and is properly installed, it is quite effective.

DOUBLE-LAYER INSTALLATION

The easiest way to achieve reduction of sound transmission is to apply a double layer of wallboard to both sides of the wall. The effectiveness can be increased by staggering the studs (**12–6**).

Double-layer screw application to steel studs also greatly increases the fire rating. The first layer is applied with the long side of the panel parallel to the studs. The second layer is screw-applied with the long edge parallel to the studs (**12–7**). The joints in the second layer must be staggered from those in the base layer and those in the panels on the other side of the wall. The first layer has screws spaced 24 inches O.C. If the second layer is to be adhesively attached, space the screws in the first layer 8 inches O.C. at joint edges 16 inches O.C. in the field.

If the second layer is ½ inch thick and the studs are 16 inches O.C. fasten to the studs with 1⅝-inch type-S screws 16 inches O.C.

SOUND-DEADENING INSULATION

The installation of insulation or sound-deadening blankets in the wall cavity further increases the sound transmission rating (**12–8**). The application of a layer of sound-deadening board to the studs before the drywall is installed is also effective (**12–9**).

After the wallboard has been installed, sound transmission can be reduced even more by caulking around any wall openings such as electrical outlets and switch boxes (**12–10**).

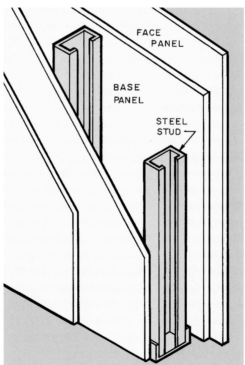

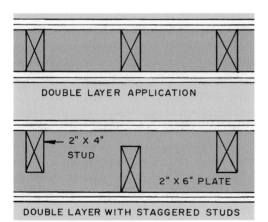

DOUBLE LAYER APPLICATION

2" X 4" STUD

2" X 6" PLATE

DOUBLE LAYER WITH STAGGERED STUDS

▲ **12–6.** Two ways used to reduce sound transmission. Either wood or metal studs can be used.

FACE PANEL

BASE PANEL

STEEL STUD

▲ **12–7.** Double-panel application reduces the amount of sound transmission and increases the fire rating of the partition.

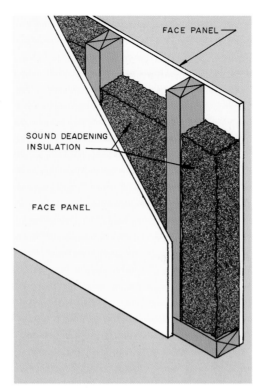

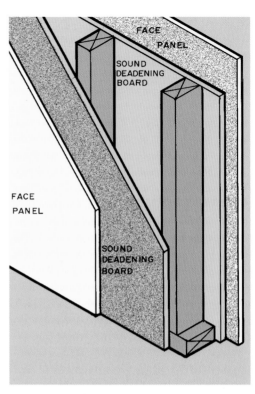

▲ **12–8.** Sound transmission through walls can be reduced by installing sound-deadening insulation blankets in the wall cavity.

▲ **12–9.** Sound-deadening board installed below the gypsum wallboard helps reduce sound transmission through the wall.

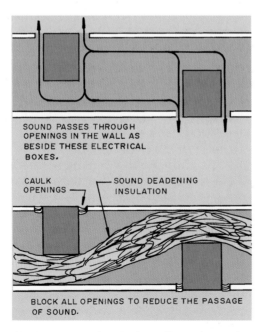

SOUND PASSES THROUGH OPENINGS IN THE WALL AS BESIDE THESE ELECTRICAL BOXES.

CAULK OPENINGS

SOUND DEADENING INSULATION

BLOCK ALL OPENINGS TO REDUCE THE PASSAGE OF SOUND.

▲ **12–10.** Openings in the wall permit sound to pass through it. Block all openings.

Fire Control

Since gypsum wallboard does not burn and resists exposure to fire, it is used to protect walls where fire danger exists or where special protection is required by codes, such as a wall between the garage and the house or between apartments. Type X drywall has special fire-resistant properties and is used as the exposed layer on these assemblies. Building codes specify the requirements that must be met. Manufacturers of gypsum products have the results of extensive tests that are used as fire-resistant walls are designed. Two examples are shown in **12–11**. Codes also specify the required nailing or screwing requirements. Double-nailing or screwing is commonly required.

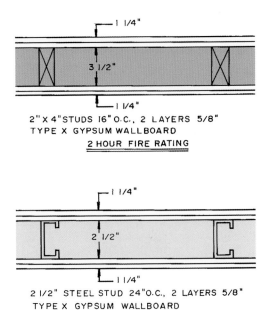

2" X 4" STUDS 16" O.C., 2 LAYERS 5/8"
TYPE X GYPSUM WALLBOARD
2 HOUR FIRE RATING

2 1/2" STEEL STUD 24" O.C., 2 LAYERS 5/8"
TYPE X GYPSUM WALLBOARD
2 HOUR FIRE RATING

▲ **12–11.** Fire ratings for two typical wall assemblies.

Exterior-Gypsum Soffit Board

Exterior gypsum soffit board is available for use on residential open porches, breezeways, carports, and exterior soffits (**12–12** and **12–13**). It has many uses on commercial buildings such as covered walkways and large canopies. These areas must be horizontal or sloping downward away from the building. Facias and moldings should be used to protect the edges from direct exposure to water. The surfaces exposed to the water should be sealed with two coats of exterior paint. The installation is the same as that used for interior ceilings.

Application to Masonry Walls

Gypsum wallboard can be applied directly to interior, above-grade concrete or masonry walls that are dry. The panels are bonded with a special adhesive available from the manufacturer. The wall

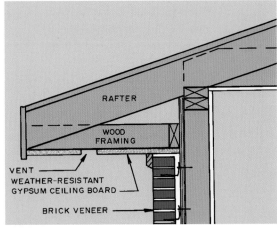

▲ **12–12.** Exterior gypsum soffit board is used for finished soffit construction.

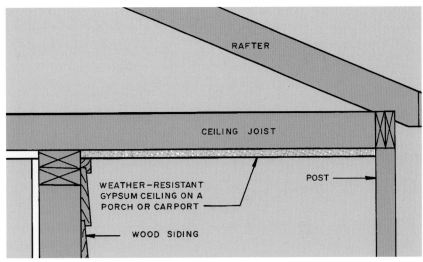

▲ **12–13.** Exterior gypsum soffit board is also used for porch and carport ceilings.

should be absolutely flat and any protruding mortar ground away. Holes should be filled with grout or a setting-type gypsum compound. Press the panels against the wall and hold them there with temporary bracing until the adhesive sets.

Below-grade masonry and concrete walls are best covered by furring out the wall with wood or steel studs and installing the drywall in the normal manner.

Application Over an Existing Wall

Gypsum wallboard can be applied over an old plaster, wallboard, or wood wall. If the old wall is smooth and sound, wallboard can be applied to it with adhesives.

Drywall nails used to hold the panel should be long enough to penetrate the framing about one inch. Screws may also be used.

When the old wall is rough or irregular, it is best to fur and shim as necessary to get a plane surface. Remember to move out and reset electrical boxes so they are flush with the face of the new wallboard.

Useful Terms for Installing Drywall

Adhesive A compound, glue, or mastic used in the application of gypsum board to framing or for laminating one or more layers of gypsum boards.

Angle A corner where two walls intersect.

Annular ring nail A deformed shank nail with improved holding qualities specially designed for use with gypsum board.

Backing board (1) A gypsum board designed for use as the first or base layer in a multilayer system. (2) A base layer in ceilings for the adhesive application of acoustical tile. (3) A type of water-resistant gypsum board.

Backup strips Pieces of wood nailed at the ceiling-sidewall corner to provide fastening for ends of plaster base or gypsum panels.

Baseboard Trim that is applied at the bottom of a wall.

Beading A condition where flat joints become visible under critical lighting, showing a narrow bead or ridge in the center of the joint. No loss of bond. Synonym for ridging and picture framing.

Bed coat First compound coat after taping.

Beveled edge The long edge of a sheet of drywall that is tapered to form a recessed area when two sheets abut.

Blister A raised loose spot on the tape caused by insufficient compound beneath the tape.

Bullnose A type of metal corner bead with rounded corners.

Butt joint Joints formed by the mill-cut ends or by job cuts without a tapered edge.

Centerline A line used as a nailing guide, running down the center of a wallboard panel.

Chalkline Straight working line made by snapping a chalked cord stretched between two points, which transfers the chalk to the work surface.

Cladding Gypsum panels, gypsum bases, gypsum sheathing, cement board, etc., applied to framing.

Corner bead A metal or plastic angle used to protect outside corners where gypsum panels meet.

Corner cracking Hairline fracture or wider crack occurring in the apex of inside corners. Synonym for shrinkage cracking and angle cracks.

Depressed nails Depressions in the joint or topping compound that occur directly over the head of a nail. Synonym for dimpled nail heads, recessed nail heads. Sometimes incorrectly referred to as shrinkage.

Drywall Generic term for interior surfacing material, such as gypsum panels, applied to framing.

Drywall lift A tool used to lift drywall to the wall and ceiling and hold it until it is nailed in place.

Drywall taping The application of tape over the gypsum wall-board joints.

Edge cracking Straight hairline cracks at one or both edges of the joint tape. Shows through finishing coats and/or painting.

Feathered edge The thin outer edge of the finish coats.

Feathering Spreading the finish coats of compound out from the joint to a very thin coating.

Fire-rated drywall Treated drywall that has a higher resistance to fire than regular drywall.

Fire wall Any wall separating two units, such as apartments.

First finishing coat Application of the first coat of joint or topping compound over tape, bead, and nails. Synonym for second coat, filling, bedding, floating, bed-coat, prebedding, first bed.

Fur down A drop-down section attached to the ceiling, such as above a set of cabinets.

Green board A gypsum panel with a green surface used in areas where dampness may be present.

Gypsum board or wallboard Generic terms for gypsum-core panels covered on both sides by paper.

High joint Butt or tapered-edge joint protruding above the plane of the board-also termed crowned.

Horizontal application Application of gypsum wallboard with the length perpendicular to the nailing members. Synonym for around the room, across the joists or studs.

Joint blisters Looseness of paper appearing after the first finishing coat.

Joint compound A compound used for taping and finishing joints in drywall construction.

Joint darkening Joint and nail spots that appear darker than the surrounding areas.

Joint lightening Joints and nail spots that appear lighter than the surrounding areas.

Joint shadowing Joints that appear darker when viewed from an oblique angle, yet show no color differentiation when seen from a right angle. Usually caused by texture variation, low joints, or high joints. Incorrectly referred to as burning, flashing, photographing, and joint darkening.

Mud A term commonly used when referring to joint compound.

Nail dimpling Depression in the wallboard surface resulting from setting nails with a wallboard hammer.

Nail-pop The protrusion of the nail usually attributed to the shrinkage of or use of improperly cured wood framing.

Predecorated wallboard A gypsum panel product that has the exposed surface finished when the panel was manufactured.

Router A power tool that uses special bits to plunge-cut interior openings within drywall panels, such as for electrical outlets or heat ducts.

Score To cut through the paper facing and into the gypsum panel.

Second finishing coat Application of the second coat of joint or topping compound over tape, bead, and nails. Synonym for third coat, finishing, finish bed, polishing, feather coat, skimming.

Shadowing An undesirable appearance that occurs when the joint finish shows through the surface decoration.

Sheen variation Joints or nail spots that appear with more or less sheen than the wallboard.

Shrinkage cracking Cracking that occurs with joint or topping compound when applied too thick in one application.

Skim coat Applications of a thin coat of joint or topping compound to the entire wall and ceiling after joint treatment. Provides a uniform smoothness of paper and joints.

Spotting nails Application of joint-finishing compound to nail heads and dimples. Synonym for spotting and nail coating.

Starved joint Depression in the joint over tapered joints. Also seen as depressions on each side of the tape on a butt joint. Synonym for low-point, delayed shrinkage, concave joint.

Substrate Underlying material to which a finish is applied or by which it is supported.

Tape photographing Outline of tape is visible in corners and flat joints after joints are finished.

Taping Application of joint compound and joint tape on gypsum wallboard joints. Synonym for embedding tape, first coat, hanging, laying tape, bedding, roughing, joint finishing.

Taping compound A joint compound designed to bond joint tape to the panel.

Texturing Application of texture by roller, spray, brush, or other method. Synonym for stripling.

Wallboard Another term for drywall.

The Metric System

AS THE CONSTRUCTION industry converts to metric units, drywall panels will be available in metric units. These sizes will be kept very close to the current inch sizes. The spacing of studs and wall height in metric units will also influence the metric wallboard panel sizes. Inch-size panels can be converted to their equivalent metric sizes by using the conversion factors in **Table 1.** This change is referred to as a soft conversion. When true metric design sizes are available, it will be referred to as hard conversion. A soft conversion of a ½-inch-thick 4 × 8 foot panel is recorded as 12.7 mm × 1201.8 mm × 2403.8 mm.

The metric system includes all aspects of measurement. The basic metric units, their symbols, and customary measuring system equivalents are shown in **Table 2.**

A table of metric equivalents is presented in **Table 3;** it is useful in the approximate quick conversion of working measurements.

TABLE 1
Metric Conversion

WHEN YOU KNOW	YOU CAN FIND	IF YOU MULTIPLY BY
Length		
inches	millimeters	25.4
feet	millimeters	300.48
yards	meters	0.91
millimeters	inches	0.04
meters	yards	1.1
Area		
square inches	square centimeters	6.45
square feet	square meters	0.09
square yards	square meters	0.83
square centimeters	square inches	0.16
square meters	square yards	1.2
Mass (Weight)		
ounces	grams	28.0
pounds	kilograms	0.45
tons (short)	metric tons	0.9
grams	ounces	0.04
kilograms	pounds	2.2
metric tons	tons (short)	1.1
Volume		
cubic feet	cubic meters	0.03
cubic inches	cubic centimeters	16.4
cubic yards	cubic meters	0.8

WHEN YOU KNOW	YOU CAN FIND	IF YOU MULTIPLY BY
Volume (Fluid)		
ounces	milliliters	30.0
pints	liters	0.47
quarts	liters	0.95
gallons	liters	3.8
milliliters	ounces	0.03
liters	pints	2.1
liters	quarts	1.06
liters	gallons	0.26
Temperature		
degrees Fahrenheit	degrees Celsius	0.6 (after subtracting 32)
degrees Celsius	degrees Fahrenheit	1.8 (then add 32)
Power		
horsepower	kilowatts	0.75
kilowatts	horsepower	1.34
Pressure		
pounds per square inch	kilopascals	6.9
kilopascals	pounds per square inch	0.15

Appendix B

Industry Trade Associations

Gypsum Association

810 First Street NE, #510
Washington, DC 20002
202-289-5440

Information Bureau for Lath, Plaster, and Drywall

3127 Los Feliz Blvd.
Los Angeles, CA 90059
231-663-2213

Wallcovering Manufacturers Association and Wallcovering
Information Bureau

401 N. Michigan Ave., Suite 2200
Chicago, IL 60611

Foundation of the Wall and Ceiling Industry

307 Annadale, Suite 200
Falls Church, VA 22042

Sterling Books by William Spence

Basic Woodworking (co-author Duane Griffiths)

Building Your Dream House

Carpentry and Building Construction: A Do-It-Yourself Guide

Constructing Bathrooms

Constructing Kitchens

Constructing Staircases, Balustrades, and Landings

Doors and Entryways

Encyclopedia of Construction Methods & Materials

Encyclopedia of Home Maintenance and Repair

Finish Carpentry: A Complete Interior & Exterior Guide

Home Carpentry and Woodworking

Installing and Finishing Drywall

Installing and Finishing Flooring

Insulating, Sealing & Ventilating Your House

Interior Trim: Making, Installing & Finishing

Residential Framing: A Homebuilder's Construction Guide

Roofing Materials and Installation

Windows and Skylights

*Woodworking Basics: The Essential Benchtop Reference
(co-author Duane Griffiths)*

About the Author

William Spence is a do-it-yourself expert who has authored more than three dozen books for Sterling Publishing Co., Inc. and for other publishers. He also has written articles for magazines and journals. Spence has been a professor of technical arts and applied sciences at Virginia Commonwealth University, Richmond, Virginia, and Western Michigan University, Kalamazoo, Michigan, as well as Chairman of the Department of Industrial Education and Art, and Dean, College of Technology, at Pittsburg State University, Pittsburg, Kansas. He has also worked in industry as General Manager and Design Draftsman for manufacturers in Virginia, has worked as a cabinetmaker, and became involved in real estate sales and land development with Sandhill Properties, Inc. of Whispering Pines, North Carolina. He earned a doctorate in education and a masters in education at the University of Missouri as well as a bachelor of science and a bachelor of science in education at Southeast Missouri State University. He also served in the United States Navy. He makes his home in Pinehurst, North Carolina, where he is currently writing technical books full time.